History of Medicine

Tony Triggs

Unwin Hyman

Acknowledgements

The author and publishers would like to thank the following for permission to reproduce photographs and illustrations:

Ancient Art and Architecture Collection 11(T) (© Ronald Sheridan) Ann Ronan Picture Library 20(R), 24(B), 25(L), 27(B), 28, 29(L) ASH 44(R) Australian Information Service, London 5(B) Barnaby's Picture Library 35(T), 40(L) BBC Hulton Picture Library 19, 30(B), 31(B). The Bodleian Library, Oxford 20(L&C) [Shelf mark 399, fol. 19R (=W.78), fol. 22R (=W.5326)] Faculty of Homeopathy 43(L) Fox Photos Ltd 34 The Health Education Authority 40(R), 44(L) The Mansell Collection 4, 10, 13(L), 17(R), 18, 23, 35(L) Mary Evans Picture Library 6(TL), 9, 30(T), 32(T), 33(B), 33(T) Milk Marketing Board 29(R) Museum of Art and History, Geneva 7 National Museum, Copenhagen 5(T), 6(TR) (© Ole Woldbye) National Portrait Gallery 26(T) Network (© Laurie Sparham) 46 Ny Carlsberg Glyptothek, Copenhagen 6(B) & TR The Photo Source 8, 15(T), 17(L), 24(T), 25(R), 27(T), 37(R), 39, 42, 43(R) Popperfoto 41B, 13(R) Punch 31, 32(B) Rex Features Ltd 47(L) University Library, Bologna 17(T) University Library Madrid (cover) Wellcome Institute Library, London 14, 26(B), 36(L&R), 37(L) World Health Organisation 9(T), 16, 38(L&R), 41(T&B), 45(T&B)

Published in 1988 by
Unwin Hyman Limited
15–17 Broadwick Street
London W1V 1FP

British Library Cataloguing in Publication Data
Triggs, Tony D.
History of medicine.
1. Medicine——History
I. Title
610′.9 R131

ISBN 0 7135 2699 8

Typeset by Latimer Trend & Company Ltd., Plymouth

Printed in Great Britain by Bell & Bain Ltd., Glasgow

Contents

To the Teacher

The past is littered with ideas and artefacts which show how the modern world came about. Civilisations build on the ruins of those gone by, and towns are shaped by the villages from which they grew. In medicine, we find that things rooted long ago in the past or deep in our psyches persist alongside superficial and recent developments. Primitive medicine is still alive and well today. We can recognise it easily in primitive cultures. Its essential features also exist in advanced societies, though familiarity blinds us to them. Illness is still attended by many taboos and rituals; its visitations still prompt recourse to authority and occultism; the link between mind and body remains very largely unfathomed.

Medicine is a subject which opens our eyes to the way we are. Pupils feel its dilemmas; they understand the challenges it has to face, and can recognise both change and continuity in its hopeless struggle with pain and death. Censorship, unbending authority, war and technology play their part in the course of the struggle. Factors like these link medicine with the whole career of man- and woman-kind on earth. Some of these factors make for change while others bring out the more primitive element. Medicine is caught in the tension between them. It claims to make progress, yet levels of malnutrition and sickness show no signs of falling.

This book is arranged chronologically, but it seeks to achieve an over-view. Through the questions and text, pupils will see the intimate links between human activity past and present. They will see how social and cultural values persist and develop; they will recognise patterns of cause and consequence, stasis and change.

As a field of study within the overall history syllabus, medicine has outstanding potential to foster a range of historical skills. The present book exploits this potential as fully as possible.

Chapter 1 Primitive medicine

By *medicine* we mean the understanding and cure of diseases and injuries. As we shall see, medical skill and knowledge have grown in a very slow, uncertain way since the earliest times.

The people who lived in caves over 10 000 years ago suffered from some of the illnesses which still affect us today. They also suffered from injuries such as broken bones. But since they did not know how to write they could not record what they thought and did about medical problems. The biggest clues we have are their bones. They prove that the cave people often suffered from *arthritis* (a painful disease affecting the joints), but we do not know if they tried to treat it in any way. However, some of these fossilised bones show the signs of *fractures* that had healed up completely. This suggests that the cave people knew the importance of keeping a broken limb as still as possible. They may have used *splints*, but we cannot be sure. It certainly seems that they cared for those who were injured and sick.

1. We know very little about what cave people thought about medicine. Why is it impossible to be sure how they treated illness and injury?

2. What clues suggest that cave people cared for those who were injured?

Limited knowledge

The cave people probably had some knowledge of what their bodies were like inside. For example, they saw the organs of people who died when wild animals tore them apart. The cave people, in turn, cut animals up in order to eat them. What they saw reinforced their sketchy knowledge about their own bodies, although animals' organs were not exactly the same as their own. They probably had very little idea of how the various organs worked. However, they knew where to plunge their spears in order to kill a struggling beast as quickly as possible. This is clear from their paintings on the walls of caves, which show animals dying with spears through their hearts.

Medicine men

The picture below was found in a cave in southern France. It looks like a man dressed up as a stag, and some people think that the man was a *witch doctor*. If this is so, it suggests that the cave people blamed evil spirits for their diseases. They probably thought that weirdly-dressed tribesmen (and pictures of them) could frighten the evil spirits away.

Cave people knew that the commonest cause of pain was an injury. But sometimes people suffered from pain without showing any signs of an injury. What could enter their bodies and do them harm without leaving a mark? The idea of evil spirits seemed an obvious answer to questions like this.

This painting was done by cave people thousands of years ago.

Letting evil spirits out

The skull is like a large container, and primitive people believed that evil spirits could live in a person's head. In order to release them, they often removed a piece of skull. This operation, known as *trepanning*, was usually done with a sharp piece of flint. It is surprising to think that anyone ever recovered from this, but skulls have been found with holes that had almost closed again. This proves that people lived for many years after having this operation.

The bits of bone removed from skulls have also been found, and some of them have a hole through the middle, suggesting that they were worn on a string like lucky charms.

A cave person's skull. You can easily see the operation he had had.

---

3. Cave people probably knew a little about *anatomy* (how the body is made up inside). What opportunities did they have to learn about this?

---

4. Evidence is the clues we can use to help us learn about the past. What are the two main types of evidence we have for cave people? What does each tell us that we can be *sure* about?

---

5. How do we think that cave people explained illness? What evidence do we have to support this?

Primitive people today

There are still some primitive people in the world today. Primitive people are those who fend for themselves in small groups and have not been affected by science and technology. Their beliefs are usually superstitious and magical. Often, these people have witch doctors to cure their diseases and curse their enemies. They also use herbs to cure illnesses, and scientists are trying to find out more about these cures before jungle clearance causes the plants and the ancient ways of life to die out.

This Australian aborigine is a witch doctor. He is putting a curse on someone. This involves pointing a sharpened bone at the victim.

---

6. Think of some strange or old-fashioned treatments which you have heard about. Do you think they worked, and if so how? What would *you* do if you had the same ailments?

Chapter 2 Medicine in ancient Egypt

Egyptian gods deciding how long human beings should live. One of the gods has a measuring stick. Perhaps each notch represents a year.

The great Egyptian doctor Imhotep

This ancient Egyptian carving shows someone affected by a bad disease called polio. What signs of this can you see?

5000 years ago one of the first great civilisations on earth lived in the Nile valley in Egypt. Every autumn the River Nile overflowed its banks, and the water and mud made the land on either side of the river extremely fertile. There was plenty of food for the farmers and other workers too, including the jewellers, tombbuilders, priests and doctors. Some of the doctors specialised in looking after particular parts of the human body (as many doctors do today). As a result, at least one of the pharaohs (or kings) of Egypt employed a whole team of doctors to care for him. There were doctors for every part of his body, including his *bowels*. The number of doctors probably matched the pharaoh's importance, but Egyptian law ensured that even the poorest people could have a doctor's help if they needed it.

Floods and blockages

Some Egyptians believed, like primitive peoples, that illness was caused by evil spirits. At medical schools attached to temples, doctors learned magical treatments to deal with these evil spirits. As a result, their prescriptions for medicine often sounded like recipes for witches' brews! For example, a potion for curing blindness included the eye of a pig, which was mashed up with other substances and then poured down the patient's ear.

Some doctors thought more deeply about the cause of diseases. One of their favourite theories was based on the River Nile and the system of dikes, canals and ditches which carried its water to faraway fields. If a waterway became blocked with mud the fields dried out. The crops shrivelled up and died, and families starved. Uncontrolled floods were also dangerous. They washed crops away, and once again many families starved.

The Egyptian doctors knew that the human body had lots of channels too. Most carried blood but some carried air and some carried food. The doctors decided that illness was caused when one of the body's pipes either burst or became blocked. Of course, certain illnesses **are** caused like this;

the Egyptian doctors' mistake was to use their ideas to explain – and treat – all sorts of conditions. They often examined their patients carefully, feeling for lumps and listening to the sound of their breathing. However, they often assumed that one of a patient's pipes had a leak or a blockage, and were trying to find which one it was. Often the trouble was totally different.

The Egyptians were especially worried about their bowels becoming blocked. They used all sorts of *laxatives* (drugs to relieve constipation) and they often finished up with diarrhoea. Perhaps we should feel sorry for the pharaoh who had a special doctor to care for his bowels!

---

1. Briefly describe two of the different theories which the Egyptians had about the cause of illness. Give an example of how the illness may have been treated in each case.

---

2. Think about the potion for curing blindness. What beliefs and attitudes does it show?

Mummification

Egyptian doctors did not know much about human anatomy. They knew that the heart sent blood to the distant parts of the body, but they seemed to think that the human heart was shaped like a cow's. In general, they made the mistake of thinking that human organs were exactly the same as those of animals. This was because they believed that the dead would need their bodies in another life. As a result, they thought it was wrong to cut bodies up to see what they were like inside. Most of their knowledge was gained by watching butchers at work. Even then, they failed to study the animals' organs with care.

Human bodies were preserved by a process called *mummification*. This did involve cutting the body open, but only so that the parts which decayed most easily could be removed. A Roman writer, Herodotus, left us a very good description of this practice:

> 'First they take a crooked piece of metal and with it draw out some of the brain through the nostrils. Then they rinse out the rest with chemicals. Next they make a cut along the side of the body with a sharp stone and take out all the digestive organs.'

The parts of the body which had been removed were placed in urns; the rest of the body was soaked in salts to stop it decaying and then wrapped in bandages.

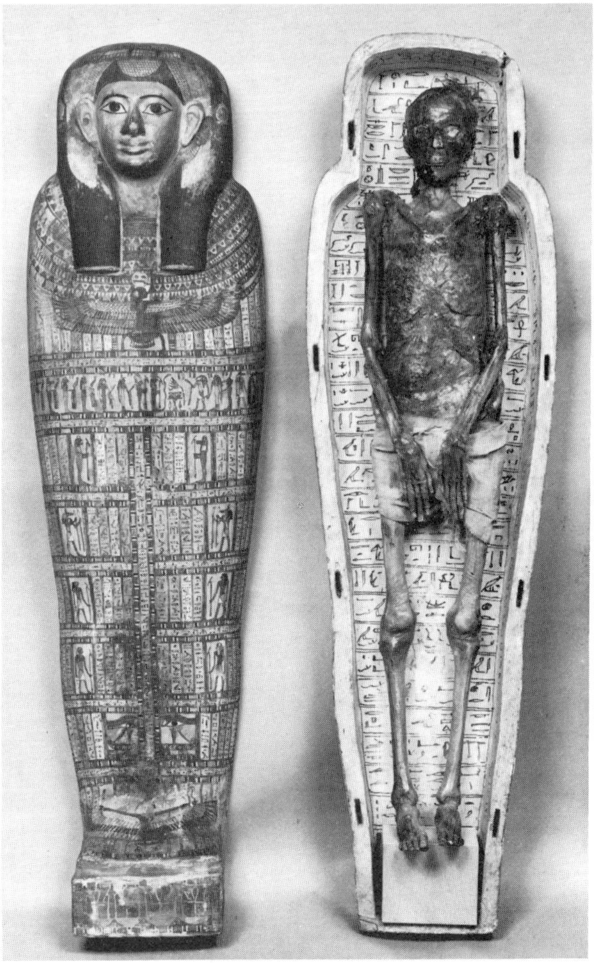

An Egyptian mummy and its case.

Mummification was done by other workers, not doctors, but even if doctors had done it themselves they would have learned little about human anatomy. They would have interpreted what they saw in accordance with all their untested theories.

---

3. What is mummification? Why did the Egyptians practise it?

---

4. Did mummification help the Egyptians to make advances in medicine? Explain your answer.

---

5. How did the Egyptians learn about anatomy?

---

6. Which branch of modern medicine needs good instruments? Do you think this branch was well advanced in ancient Egypt? Give reasons for your answer.

Chapter 3 The Greek healing temple

A reconstruction of the scene in one of the Greek healing temples. The statue is of the god Aesculapius.

As we have seen, religion and magic were – and are – extremely important in primitive medicine. They played a smaller part in the medicine of ancient Egypt, but were still important to many people. In ancient Greece (that is to say, in Greece over 2000 years ago) there were two distinct views of medicine and healing. One view emphasised the part which the gods played in illness and healing. The other view was more scientific: according to this, diseases have their causes in the natural world (including the body). Healing, too, was regarded as a natural process; it might be assisted by medical skill but not by magic.

In this chapter we shall look at ideas and practices which were based on Greek religion and magic. In particular, we shall look at what was done at the *aesculapia* (healing temples). They were named after a doctor called Asklepios (or Aesculapius), whom people had come to regard as a god. Many aesculapia were built in his honour, and people went there hoping that he and the other gods would cure their illnesses.

Cleansing and cure

Bathing in spring water often formed part of the treatment at the aesculapia. This may have been good for the patients' health, especially if the water was rich in salts and minerals. They bathed for religious reasons too. They hoped that the water would cleanse their souls as well as their bodies. They wanted to wash away all the guilt and evil inside them, for they thought that the gods had punished them with illnesses because of their sins.

The cleansing process could take several days, and during this time they had the chance to read inscriptions cut on stone tablets and set in the walls of the temple. They described cures which had taken place in previous years.

When a priest decided that a patient was ready he led him or her inside to pray at the altar. He then led the patient into the innermost part of the temple. This was like a hospital ward with piles of animal skins laid out on the floor as bedding. Here the patients were given drugs to make them sleep, and snakes were allowed to slither across the patients' bodies, touching them with their flickering tongues. These sacred snakes were supposed to aid the process of healing. Sure enough, most of the patients woke up cured of whatever was wrong with them. Any who still complained of illness were told by the priests that their faith in the gods had not been sufficient. Only those who trusted the gods and the priestly magic could hope to be cured.

We know about the temples because the ruins still exist today, and some of the tablets describing cures can still be read. According to one tablet,

> 'Euippos had had for six years the point of a spear in his cheek. As he was sleeping the god extracted the spear-head and put it in his hands.'

We also know about the temples from ancient books and plays. One play describes how a blind man was cured by two huge snakes which licked his eyelids during the night.

---

1. Pits have been found at some of the temples. What do you think these pits were for?

---

2. Pretend that you are a patient at an aesculapian temple. Write two or three paragraphs describing your experience.

Healing the mind

No one today believes in Aesculapius and the other Greek gods, and few believe in the healing power of the yellow snakes. Because of this, it is hard to understand why so many cures occurred.

An artist's impression of the scene outside an Aesculapian temple.

The symbol of the World Health Organisation. Whose snake and staff appear in the symbol?

However, the Greeks were right in saying that faith was what mattered. The Greeks put their faith in priests, gods and sacred snakes; a modern patient will probably trust a doctor or a particular medicine. The important thing is the patient's **belief** that he or she will be cured. The reason for this is that many illnesses start in the mind. For example, indigestion and sleeplessness are often caused by anxiety. If a patient believes that a certain form of treatment will work he will worry less about his health and may start to get better.

The importance of faith

When we look again at what went on in the aesculapia we can see that everything done there helped to ease the conflicts and problems in the patients' minds. Bathing must have been very relaxing in itself, and because of its religious meaning it helped the patients to get rid of all their feelings of guilt. Reading about the cures that had already taken place made them sure that they too would be cured. Inside the temple the drugs which they were given relaxed them and helped them to feel more confident. They were now in one of their holiest places; they believed that the gods had forgiven their sins and they knew that they would soon be tended by priests whose snakes had mysterious powers. For many patients, their improved state of mind ensured that their symptoms would soon disappear.

---

3. Explain the importance of (a) bathing, (b) reading and (c) drugs in the healings at the aesculapia. Do you think that there would have been as many healings if the patients had slept outside in huts? Why?

---

4. How did the Greeks think the cures at the aesculapia happened? How do *you* think they happened?

Chapter 4 Hippocrates

As well as aesculapian priests there were plenty of doctors and midwives in Greece, and they usually treated illness with drugs. In the earliest times they used the drugs like magical potions, with little real understanding either of illness or of particular symptoms. Like the priests, they blamed mysterious forces for things which they could not understand.

However, 2400 years ago a Greek doctor called Hippocrates questioned the old superstitious ideas. For example, he contradicted the view that epileptic fits were due to a god or spirit taking charge of the sufferer's brain.

> 'Epilepsy is not, in my view, any more divine or sacred than any other disease, but has a natural cause. Its supposed divine origin is due to men's inexperience, and to their wonder at its peculiar character. Each disease has a natural cause.'

He went on to say that these natural causes of illness include bad diet, unhealthy living conditions and weaknesses which are present at birth.

Hippocrates stressed the part which nature plays in recovery. If a doctor acts too hastily he may interfere with natural healing. He must take the time to examine the patient carefully, and must always check the following points:

- What sort of night has the patient had?
- Are his bowels functioning?
- What are his sweat and *urine* like?
- Does he feel hot?
- What sounds are obtained by tapping his body? What do these sounds indicate about his liver and other organs?
- What can be learned by listening to the patient's chest?

1. What was new in Hippocrates' ideas about the causes of illness?

2. According to Hippocrates, why should doctors avoid acting hastily? What should they do first?

3. Give an example of:
(a) a question Hippocrates would ask a patient
(b) how he would use his eyes
(c) how he would use his hands
(d) how he would use his ears.

Hippocrates.

Dealing with causes

Let us suppose that a patient is coughing repeatedly because he needs to clear some *phlegm* or other substance from his throat. The following list shows three different ways of helping this patient:

1. The primitive way:
The cough is an evil spirit barking. We must scare the evil spirit away.
2. A common way:
We must give this patient medicine in order to stop him coughing.
3. Hippocrates' way:
We must listen carefully and find out what is causing the cough before treating it. For example,

> 'if there is pain in the chest and a sound is heard like leather rubbing against leather the patient has pleurisy [inflammation of the outer lining of the lungs].'

Whatever the problem, Hippocrates encouraged doctors to find the cause and treat it. He believed in selecting drugs with care, and that operations should only be carried out when the chances of success were good.

Hippocrates founded a medical school on the Greek island of Cos and his pupils helped to spread his ideas. Before setting out, each new trainee swore a solemn oath which bound him to do his medical work to the best of his ability. The oath included the following words:

> 'I shall administer no poison to any person, even at their request. I shall never give a woman anything to cause an abortion. When I enter a house I shall go there for the healing of the sick, and I shall abstain from doing anything wicked or wrong.'

The oath is still well-known today. It is called the Hippocratic Oath, and doctors try to follow the very high standards it sets.

4. Look again at the different ways of dealing with coughs. How might Hippocrates have criticised methods 1 and 2?

5. How did Hippocrates try to spread his ideas? How is his influence still felt today?

The theory of humours

Hippocrates' work had certain weaknesses. Like the Egyptians, the Greeks thought it wrong to dissect human bodies. As a result, Hippocrates and his students did not know much about human anatomy. Another weakness was the emphasis which they placed on ideas of balance and harmony. To some extent they were perfectly right: for example, we know that a balanced diet is vital to a person's health. However, these early doctors applied ideas of balance to everything. One, called Alcmaeon, said that health depended on opposites such as hot and cold, wet and dry, and sweet and sour being balanced exactly inside the body. If they were not then illness would follow. Another doctor called Philolaus said that just as the earth has a fire at its centre so the human body has heat at its centre. He claimed that the

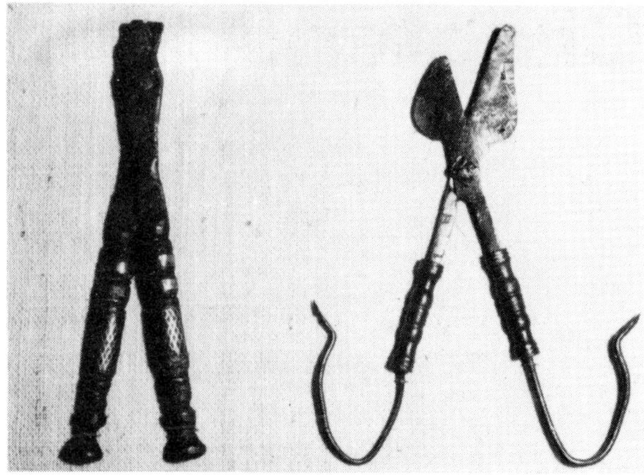

Surgical instruments used by doctors in ancient Greece.

body needs cooling air to balance this heat.

The most detailed idea about balance was called the theory of *humours*. According to this, the world was made of air, water, fire and earth and the body contains four corresponding humours or fluids: blood, phlegm, yellow bile and black bile.

> 'Man is healthy when these elements are correctly adjusted to each other, both in strength and amount, and are well mixed. Sickness occurs when one of them is present in an inadequate or excessive amount, or is isolated in the body and fails to combine with the rest.'

These wrong ideas did not interfere excessively with the medical treatment the Greek doctors gave, but they hindered the progress of medical thought for many centuries.

6. Copy the diagram below and fill in the blanks.

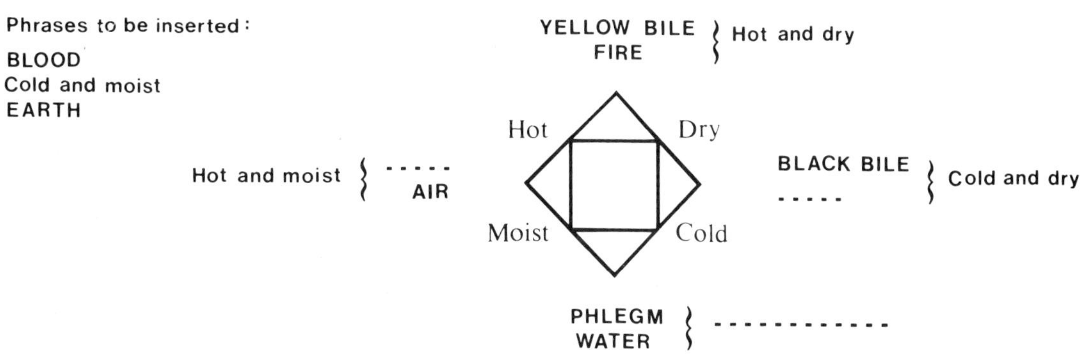

The Greeks believed that everything fitted into a pattern.

Chapter 5 Roman medicine and public health

About 2000 years ago the Romans conquered Greece and the other Greek-speaking lands at the eastern end of the Mediterranean. The Romans had never thought very deeply about diseases or medical treatment, and they did not pay much attention to the work of Hippocrates and the doctors who followed him. The Romans were generally satisfied with simple medicines which every household could make for itself. For example, they tried to cure diarrhoea by dosing themselves with egg-yolk mixed with powdered eggshell, wine and poppy-juice. This was probably quite a good treatment. The wine and the juice had a sedative (or calming) effect, and the egg-yolk and egg-shell settled their stomachs.

The Romans' real success was in *preventive medicine*. In other words, they did things to stop diseases from happening. They began by tackling diarrhoea and malaria, for these were very common in Rome. But why were they common? The Romans realised that both were connected in some way with the swampy land near the city. They therefore set about draining the swamps and quickly found that their health was improving. As usual, the Romans had shown themselves to be people of action; they had not tried to gain a full understanding of why the swamps were so unhealthy, though some of their theories were nearly correct (see the following chart).

1. What is meant by preventive medicine?

2. Which illnesses were common in Rome? What did the Romans do about them?

3. Look at the table. What did all the Romans agree about? What did they disagree about?

4. How did malaria get its name? (A good dictionary will probably help you.)

Gods, doctors and water supplies

As we have seen, the Romans' outlook was practical rather than scientific, and this meant that they were confused by any new turn of events. When epidemics of plague struck Rome the inhabitants turned to the pagan gods, and they built an aesculapian temple. They employed Greek doctors to help them deal with other diseases but they sometimes felt that the doctors were useless, especially when they quarrelled about the correct form of treatment. One or two dying people complained that the doctors who crowded round their bed had done them more harm than the illness itself!

Not surprisingly, the Romans continued to concentrate on preventive medicine. When they built new cities, villages and fortresses they avoided marshes and stagnant water, choosing instead

Some Romans said that swamps caused diseases by giving off poisonous gases.

Some Romans said that the swamps bred creatures too small to see which caused their health problems.

Some Romans said that the swamps bred insects whose stings caused diseases.

Together, these Romans were very near to the modern idea of airborne germs (bacteria).

Together, these Romans were very near to the truth about malaria, which is caused by tiny organisms and spread by the bites of infected mosquitoes.

places with plenty of fresh air and springs. They tested the water by boiling a sample in a cauldron. If there was no deposit left when all the water had boiled away, it was probably safe. They also checked the health of local people. If they were fit and strong, the Romans felt sure that they too could live in the area safely and drink the same water.

As their empire grew bigger, the Romans were sometimes forced to live in places with insufficient good water. They solved the problem by building conduits (channels) along which water supplies flowed from sources far away in the hills.

Rome itself had several such conduits, with a total length of over 200 kilometres. Some of the water was needed to cleanse Rome's underground sewers. These carried waste from the many flush toilets in public places and private homes. Hygienic toilet and sewage arrangements helped to keep Roman citizens healthy.

Baths and hospitals

The Romans also needed water for public baths. They used their baths for recreation and to treat certain illnesses. However, keeping fit and clean was the most important reason for bathing; as we have seen, the Romans believed in preventing illness rather than curing it.

The Romans did build hospitals, but these were mainly for wounded soldiers. The staff were also soldiers who knew how to deal with battle wounds.

5. What did the Romans do to ensure that their water supplies were safe and plentiful? What did they use the water for?

6. What did hospitals concentrate on in Roman times? Why do you think they were mostly built near the boundaries of the Roman Empire?

This Roman aqueduct (or bridge for carrying water) can still be seen at Nîmes in France.

Roman baths.

Chapter 6 Galen

GALENI
LIBRORVM
PRIMA CLASSIS
NATVRAM CORPORIS HVMANI,
hoc est elementa, temperaturas, humores,
structuræ habitudinis q; modos, partium
anatomias, vsus, facultates & actiones,
seminis denique fœtuum que tra-
ctationes, complectens:
QVARTA HAC NOSTRA EDITIONE,
VENETIIS APVD IVNTAS M D LXV.

The title page of an edition of Galen's works published in 1565. By that time, Galen's ideas had been studied and believed for 1400 years.

Apart from Hippocrates, Galen was the greatest of the ancient Greek doctors. He was born in AD 131 at Pergamon in Asia Minor (modern Turkey). In Galen's time this was one of the Greek-speaking areas ruled by the Romans.

After studying medicine, Galen gained valuable experience as doctor to the gladiators who fought in the arena at Pergamon. Their sword fights resulted in severed nerves and arteries, and Galen saw that serious injuries often led to symptoms like paralysis. He guessed that many diseases were linked to damage which somehow occurred in the body. However, he also believed the traditional theory of humours.

Galen believed, like Hippocrates, in the careful observation of symptoms. However, he went much further than Hippocrates, for he carried out experiments and observed the results. He performed some of these on living animals, in spite of the terrible pain this caused. For example, he took a pig, opened it up and tied the pipes that came from its kidneys. He then watched the kidneys swell because the *urine* they made could not escape. He also cut a pig's spinal nerve at various places along its back. A cut near the tail paralysed the pig's hind legs; a cut higher up affected a larger part of its body, preventing it from breathing and squealing; a cut at the neck caused total paralysis. Galen was learning exactly where different nerves branched out from the spinal cord. He rightly guessed that the human body was similar, and the knowledge he gained was useful to him in dealing with his patients' complaints.

Galen went to Rome and became the city's most famous doctor—one of the few whom people would trust. He impressed the Romans by curing patients whom other doctors had failed to cure. For example, a Persian philosopher who lived in Rome was suffering from numbness in three of his fingers. Other doctors had given him various ointments but Galen asked him if he had had any injuries. The Persian replied that he had hit the upper part of his back on a sharp piece of rock. Galen said that he must have damaged his spine in the place where the finger nerves branch off. He told the man to rest in bed and apply his ointment to his back. Sure enough, the feeling soon came back to his fingers.

In spite of his cleverness, Galen's treatments often depended on the idea of balance. He chilled patients suffering from fever and sometimes gave pepper to people whose ailments were due to cold weather.

---

1. What work did Galen do at Pergamon? What did it teach him?

---

2. What did Galen do
(a) to the pipes that led from a pig's kidneys?
(b) to a pig's spinal cord?
In each case say what Galen noticed and why it occurred.

---

3. Explain why some doctors told the philosopher to put ointment on his fingers but Galen told him to put it on his back.

---

4. Look again at page 10. Which of the three approaches to illness helped the philosopher?

The heart and the blood supply

Galen dissected many dead animals. Like the Egyptians, people in the Roman Empire believed that the dead would need their bodies in another life, so Galen could not dissect human beings. However, he sometimes had the chance to examine a rotting corpse or a skeleton, and he always learned as much as he could. He gained an excellent understanding of human anatomy but

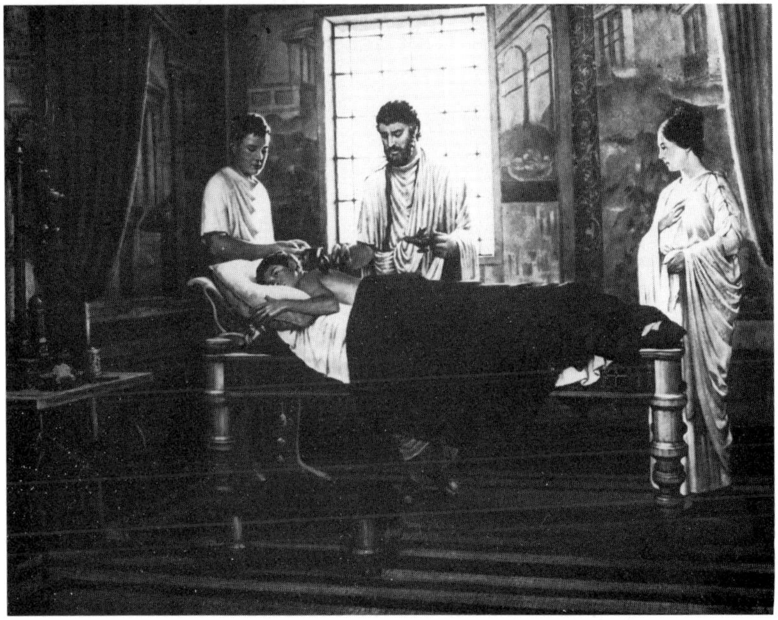

Galen treating a patient.

his understanding of *physiology* (the way the various organs work) was rather limited.

Nowadays we know that though the heart has two separate sides it circulates one lot of blood round the body. Galen believed there were two lots of blood. He said that blood from the right-hand side of the heart flowed to the lungs and the liver and then flowed back. In a similar way, blood from the left-hand side of the heart served the rest of the body.

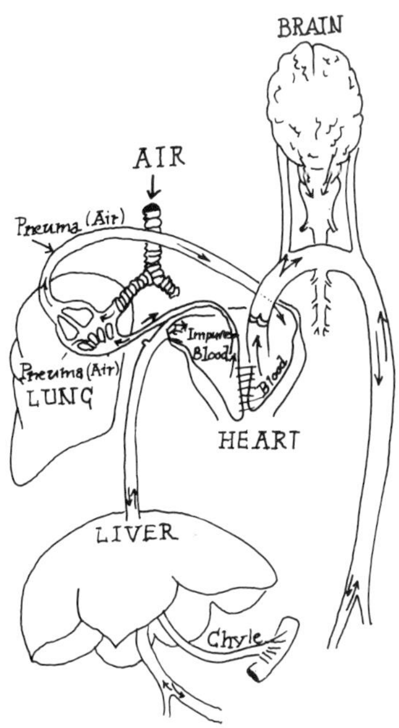

Galen's idea of how blood moves inside the body.

Galen did not think that the two lots of blood were **totally** separate; he believed that some mixing occurred by means of some tiny pipes which linked the two systems. For example, he said (mistakenly) that a little blood could pass from the right of the heart to the left through invisible pores in the central wall. Galen believed that some of the blood was used up when it reached the limbs and bodily organs. He also believed that the liver made new blood from food.

People believed Galen's wrong ideas for over 1000 years. This prevented medical progress. It also prevented the understanding and treatment of many illnesses, especially circulatory problems like varicose veins. The Church was largely to blame because it taught that Galen's work was correct. It approved of Galen's view that every natural thing had a definite purpose; this agreed with the Church's idea of God as a sort of almighty designer. Galen's outlook also appealed to Hebrew and Arab religious thinkers.

So great was the power of religion in the period stretching from ancient times to the late Middle Ages that few people dared to disagree with anything that Galen had written. Moreover the ban on dissections made it hard to discover all his mistakes.

5. Galen was wrong about a number of things. Give some examples.

6. How did religion hinder medical progress?

Chapter 7 Medicine in the Muslim world

An Arab doctor sealing a wound by putting a very hot iron against it.

The Christian church encouraged healing through faith, prayer and careful nursing, and in this way it continued the word of the Greek aesculapia. In some respects the work was extended, for the Christian healing institutions cared for orphans and elderly people as well as the sick. Lengthy stays were often involved and prayer was considered of vital importance. These places slowly turned into monasteries, and for hundreds of years the monks were among the very few people who preserved and studied the medical books by the ancient authors.

However, these books were also preserved by Arabic-speaking scholars from Spain, north Africa and the Middle East. These scholars believed in the Muslim faith. Its founder, Mohammed, had lived in Arabia, but after his death in 632 his followers conquered an empire extending from Spain in the west to Persia (modern Iran) in the east. Here, at a place called Gondishapur, the empire's finest scholars translated the medical books from Greek into Arabic.

Translating Greek texts

The work of translation continued throughout the 8th and 9th centuries. It speeded up when the Empire's rulers built themselves a capital city at Baghdad in Iraq. Among the magnificent buildings were a library and a hospital. These attracted doctors and scholars from many parts of the Muslim world. They were eager to translate and study the works of Galen and Hippocrates. However, copies were very scarce, even in Greece. To make matters worse, Greece belonged to the Byzantine Empire ruled by the Muslims' enemies, the Christians. As a result, the Muslims could not get books from Greece, but had to obtain them from other lands. One scholar searched the whole Middle East for a book by Galen and found only half of it. In the end, though, scholars were able to translate all the works of Galen and Hippocrates as well as those of other Greeks. They also wrote some books of their own, including the first-ever study of the human eye.

---

1. How were medical books preserved
(a) in Europe?
(b) in the Muslim Empire?

---

2. Why was it so difficult for medical scholars in the Muslim Empire to learn from the work of Greek and Roman doctors?

Doctors under Muslim rule

Doctors in the lands under Muslim rule were highly respected, though bad ones could suffer serious punishments. Most doctors treated the poor without charge, though they earned enormous sums from their wealthy patients. They worked out what to do for their patients in various ways: some used astrological methods but most examined their patients' urine and checked their pulse. Drugs were the commonest form of treatment, but magic was also used at times. For example, prescriptions were often written with *laxative* juices instead of ink. This may have helped patients by giving them extra faith in the treatment. Encouraging words could also do this. 'Comfort the sufferer with the promise of healing, for in that way you aid his natural powers,' wrote one Muslim doctor.

Rhazes and Avicenna

Rhazes was a doctor who lived and worked in Baghdad at the start of the 10th century. He

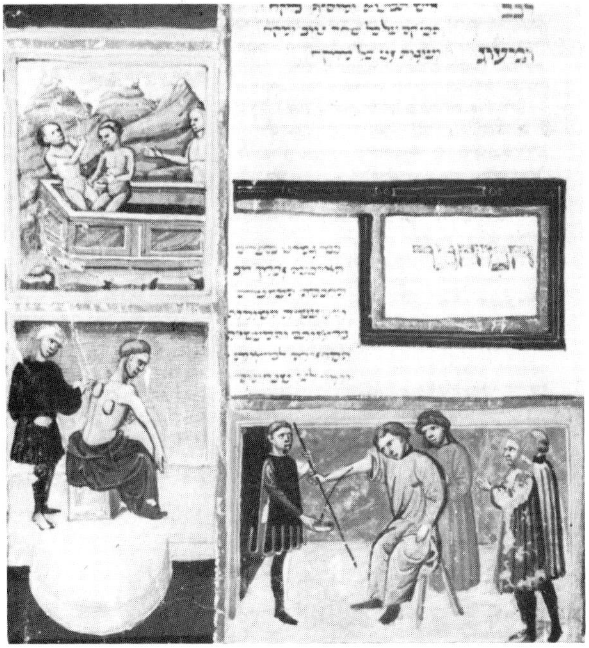

Part of a 17th century Hebrew translation of Avicenna's work.

emphasised the importance of observation and experience. He described the symptoms of small-pox and measles; he also gave advice on the treatment of certain conditions. To lessen a fever he recommended cooling the patient's body with water.

A hundred years later, a Persian doctor called Avicenna wrote books in which he repeated the views of earlier doctors. For example, his *Canon* was based on the work of Hippocrates and Galen.

An artist's impression of Avicenna writing his Canon.

In spite of this, the *Canon* has an important place in medical history. This is because translations of it were the principal medical textbooks in Europe until the 17th century.

Albucasis the surgeon

In some ways Cordoba in Spain was even more advanced than Baghdad. It eventually had about 70 libraries and 50 hospitals. Surgery had long been neglected by doctors under Muslim rule, partly because of religious restrictions. However, Spain had separate rulers who encouraged surgery. The greatest Spanish surgeon was a Cordoban called Albucasis, who lived and worked in the 10th century. He wrote about the skills of the midwife and dentist. He also described the instruments and skills that were needed for major surgery. He knew two ways of closing wounds: one was to sew the edges together; the other was to bring them together by hand and then make insects nip them with their jaws or pincers. If the rest of the insect was broken off the jaws or the pincers stayed in place.

Albucasis felt the need for a greater knowledge of human anatomy. He also realised that pain, bleeding and infected wounds often led to his patients' death. As we shall see later, the problems he faced were not solved until the 19th and 20th centuries. At least Albucasis cut his patients open in the right ways – and usually for the right reasons. Like other Muslims he played his part in passing medical knowledge on to the doctors of Europe.

---

3. Write a brief note about why you think each of the following was important:
(a) Rhazes (b) Avicenna (c) Albucasis.

Arab doctors examine a patient.

Chapter 8 Medicine in Medieval Europe (1)

For 600 years, from the 5th century to the 11th century, medicine in Europe made almost no progress, for people relied on remedies which were handed down from father to son and from mother to daughter. They also trusted ancient authors like Galen and Hippocrates, though they did not always know their work well.

Some traditional treatments probably worked, especially the ones that were based on herbs. A favourite medicinal plant was the *mandrake*. People used the juice from the roots to deaden pain and send them to sleep. The mandrake plant was thought to be magical. Its roots were forked, and they often resembled a human body with arms and legs. People believed that when the plant was pulled from the soil it shrieked with pain, and that if a person pulled one up he would die or go mad. Because of this, the roots were gathered in special ways. One writer said that people should start by digging around a plant to loosen it.

> 'Then, when you see its hands and feet, tie a piece of string to it. Tie the other end of the string round the neck of a hungry dog. Throw meat in front of the dog so that it cannot reach it without pulling up the mandrake.'

In this way people could get the roots without really pulling them up themselves.

Superstitious beliefs increased the effect of herbal remedies. They made them seem more special, and this meant that patients trusted them more.

Medicine in monasteries

As well as being practised by families, medicine was also practised by monks. Monastery buildings included a small infirmary where monks and other sick people were cared for. The monks grew herbs in the monastery grounds, and they used these herbs to treat the sick. However, they felt that healing was really the work of God, so faith and prayer were the most important part of the treatment.

The monks did not study people's symptoms with very much care. They felt that God could heal any disease, so the meaning of symptoms could be ignored.

---

1. Compare the ways in which families and monks treated illnesses. How were they similar? How were they different?

---

2. In what ways was the treatment in monasteries similar to that in aesculapia?

---

3. How did the monks' beliefs interfere with medical progress?

The School of Salerno

In the 9th century a medical school was opened at a place called Salerno in Italy. No one knows how the school began. However, it was a centre for people (including monks) who felt that herbs and faith could not cure every case.

The school attracted many great scholars. One of the most important of these was a man called Constantinus the African. He came to the school in the 11th century, after living in northern Africa and the Middle East. He worked at trans-

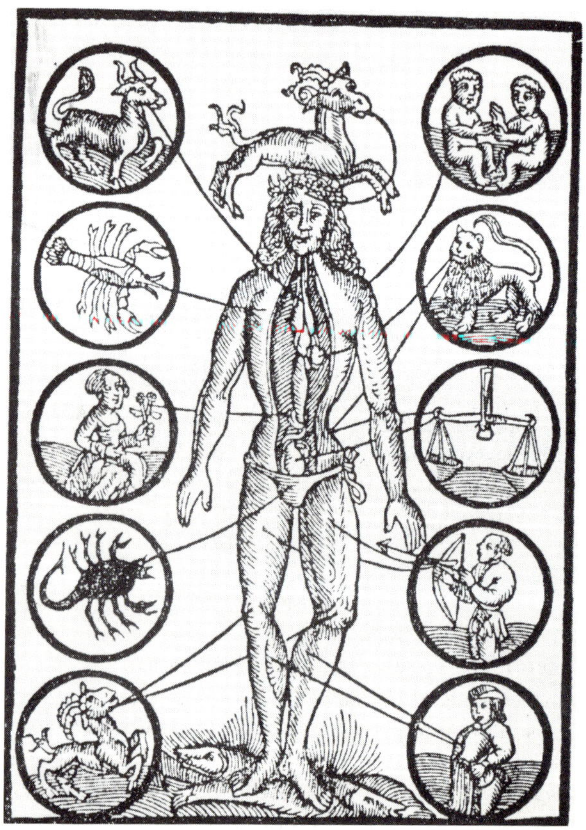

A 'Zodiac chart' (see the opposite page).

lating medical works from Arabic into Latin (the language used by scholars in Europe). Monks and scholars already had a few translations of medical works by the ancient Greeks. Now they could see what Muslim doctors like Avicenna thought of these works.

The task of translating continued during the following century. Many translations contained ideas which stimulated medical thinking, and schools like the one at Salerno were founded at several places in Western Europe. These medical schools trained doctors and midwives, and many produced important medical books of their own. At the same time the medical work of the monasteries slowly died out.

Obtaining leeches for medical use.

Urine charts and 'zodiac charts'

Unlike the monks, medieval doctors thought *diagnosis* was very important. They examined their patients in all the ways which Hippocrates had recommended (see Chapter 4). They inspected their patients' urine with particular care, checking its colour against the shades on a special chart. They did this because they wrongly supposed that every shade had a definite meaning. If an operation was needed the doctor would use a 'zodiac chart' to find a safe date. The chart depicted a human figure with signs to show which constellations (or groups of stars) were thought to 'rule' different parts of the body. Each part had to be left alone during the month when its stars were high in the sky. Thus, like doctors from earlier times, medieval doctors and surgeons examined their patients carefully, but diagnosed and treated diseases in ways which we would consider strange.

4. Say briefly why the monks' way of healing differed from the doctors'.

5. What do the 'zodiac chart' and the quote about mandrake tell us about the state of scientific thought and treatment outside the monastries?

Effects of Greek influence

Though the new translations stimulated medical progress they also reinforced some very old mistakes. This was because the Muslim doctors supported Greek ideas about bodily humours. Blood was one of the bodily humours and many diseases were thought to result from excessive amounts of it in the body. Doctors and surgeons had various ways of removing this excess blood. Blood-sucking leeches were used to remove small quantities. Moderate amounts were removed by *cupping*. This involved making a tiny cut on the patient's body and covering it with a heated 'cup' or vessel. The vessel remained in place by suction and drew out some of the patient's blood. Finally, large amounts of blood were released by cutting open a vein.

The effects of Greek ideas were felt in other ways too, for the Muslim writers agreed with Galen that *pus* must appear before wounds can heal. This was an understandable error. Usually, the open wounds which were caused by operations and accidents festered (became infected) after two or three days. Pus which appeared in the wound was the result of the body's fight against dirt and disease. It was a waste product but no one understood this. All they knew was that some patients died but many recovered, and Galen had thought that the pus in some way assisted their healing.

6. How did the work of Constantinus the African affect the advance of medicine?

7. Why was bleeding done? What were the three methods of bleeding? Which pictures in chapters 6 and 7 show patients being bled? In each case say which method was being used.

Chapter 9 Medicine in Medieval Europe (2)

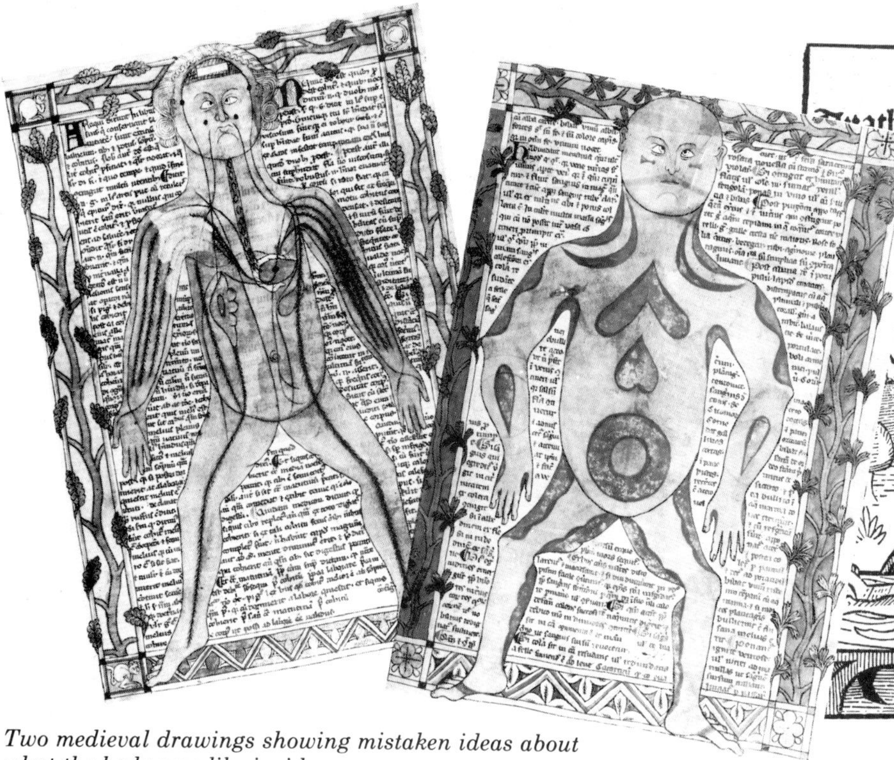

Two medieval drawings showing mistaken ideas about what the body was like inside.

A medical student dissecting a corpse. His teacher is using a book to explain how everything works. (Is this a good thing?)

In the 13th century, two doctors who were trained at Salerno disputed Galen's idea that pus was good. These doctors, Hugh de Lucca and his son Theodoric, pointed out that if a wound is carefully and promptly closed no pus will appear and healing will take place rapidly. Another doctor called Henri de Mondeville criticised surgeons for getting dirt into patients' wounds. He wrote, 'Many more surgeons know how to cause *suppuration* (festering) than to heal a wound'.

Hugh de Lucca gained experience in dealing with wounds when he worked as an army doctor. De Lucca found that alcoholic drinks like wine could be put on wounds to prevent them festering. Poor people found that mouldy bread had the same effect. Clearly, these people no longer thought suppuration was good. However, they had no idea that the alcohol and mould were killing tiny living things in their wounds. As we shall see, people did not understand about germs for several centuries, and germ-killing medicine was not mass-produced from mould until the 1940s (see Chapter 18).

Anatomy and surgery

In the early part of the 14th century, anatomists began to insist on making human *dissections*. Some anatomists obtained their corpses from battlefields while others, like the Italian Mondino, obtained the bodies of criminals from the gallows. Despite the growth of anatomical knowledge, doctors remained confused about *physiology*. For example, they failed to realise that blood is circulated round the body.

Aided by Mondino's anatomical studies, a French surgeon called de Chauliac performed operations with great success. Good anaesthetics had not been invented, but de Chauliac used a mixture of drugs to make patients drowsy before operations. These included juices from plants like the mandrake and poppy. Some patients swallowed the mixture, while others breathed the fumes from a sponge.

1. **Look back to the end of Chapter 8. In what way did de Lucca disagree with Galen about the healing of wounds?**

2. **Why had anatomists not been able to make human dissections before the 14th century? Where did they now get their corpses from?**

3. **How did de Chauliac partly solve one of the main problems Albucasis had met? (Look back to Chapter 7.)**

Back-street surgery

Although leading surgeons were learning that festering hindered recovery, most surgeons either did not know or did not care about keeping wounds clean. Many were simply doctors' assistants, badly trained and doing the messiest parts of the work. Many other surgeons were barbers, earning most of their money by cutting hair and trimming beards. They also extracted rotting teeth and carried out simple operations like letting blood. They used the same tools for various jobs and they did not know how important it was to keep them clean. In any case, like other people who lived at the time, they did not even have clean running water.

4. **(a) Give some reasons why barbers did not make very good doctors.**
(b) Barbers had a special sign outside their shops called a barber's pole. It can still be seen at a few men's hairdressers. Find out what the sign is like and what it represents.

'Carrion and stinking filth'

The work of the finest doctors, surgeons and anatomists was not yet having much effect on the general standard of medical practice and public health. Ideas spread slowly, for efficient methods of printing were not introduced until the middle of the 15th century. In any case, low standards of *hygiene* could not be changed quickly.

Nowadays, there are many hygiene regulations, covering things like water supplies and sewage disposal. In medieval times the regulations were few in number and hard to enforce. For example, there were fines for depositing 'dunghills, carrion and other stinking filth in the highway', but since few cities had sewers or means of rubbish disposal people were forced to use the streets.

Dangerous food

Food was often of very poor quality. Meat was especially dangerous to health. Refrigerators had not been invented, and butchers kept all their meat on show. In warm weather the meat attracted flies from the heaps of dung and rubbish in the street. A London by-law said that butchers were not allowed to sell meat that was 'putrid, rotten, and an abomination to the human race'. People complained of

> 'Putrid blood running down the streets, abominable and most filthy stinks . . . , sickness and many other evils . . . and great dangers for the time to come.'

Fears like this were justified, for in 1348 *plague* swept through Europe killing at least a third of the people.

5. **In what ways was city life unhealthy just before the plague began?**

6. **Look again at Chapter 5. How might the Romans have improved the hygiene conditions described in the present chapter?**

7. **Look at the plan of Fountains Abbey, Yorkshire, in the 14th century. How do you think the river was used to safeguard health? Try to pick out another feature which you think was either healthy or unhealthy.**

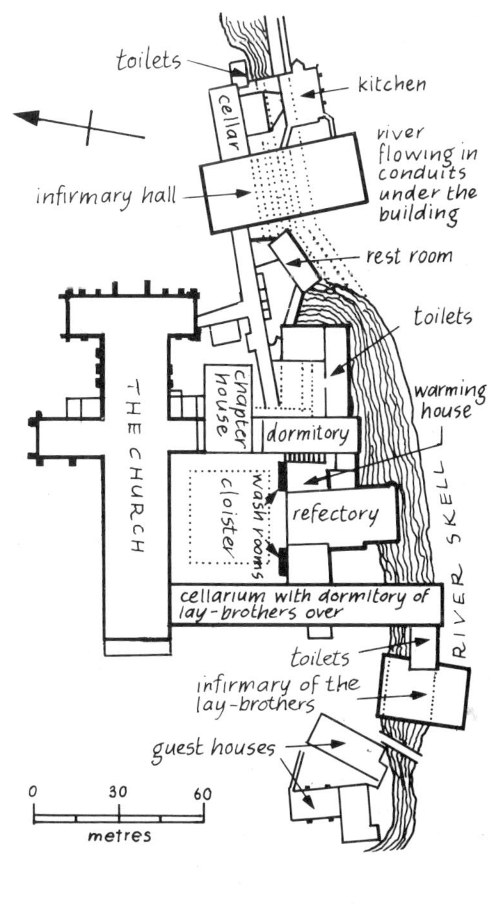

Chapter 10 The Black Death

Death seizes a merchant.

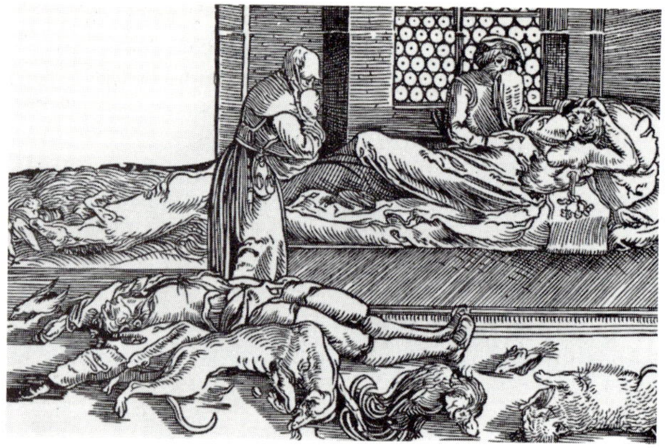

Trying to save a dying man.

Some medieval doctors seemed to have little faith in their own methods and treatment, and this often destroyed their patients' trust. During epidemics of fatal diseases many people simply panicked, while doctors argued among themselves about what they should do. The panic and disagreement reached a climax during the plague (or Black Death) which swept across Europe in 1348 and 1349. A 14th century medical textbook said that there were two kinds of plague:

> 'The first [caused] fever and spitting of blood, and the victims were dead within three days. The second [caused] fever but with swellings and boils, particularly in the armpit and groin. This form of plague took five days to kill.'

A witness called Giovanni Boccaccio recorded that

> 'black or reddish spots appeared on the arm, the thigh or in other places. . . . And just as the swellings had been an unfailing sign of approaching death so were the spots.'

When we study what people said and did at the time of the plague we can see that many correct ideas about the cause and control of disease were mixed up with false ones. For example, many doctors fled from cities to homes in the countryside. They obviously knew that filth and overcrowding were dangerous.

Isolating plague victims

At the time of the plague, people did not understand about germs but they knew that most diseases were catching. Some town councils therefore made strict rules to keep the infection out. Under these rules, travellers were not allowed to enter the town until they had waited outside its walls for a month or so. This period, known as *quarantine*, ensured that if people had the disease they died outside the town walls, instead of bringing in the infection. Unfortunately, the plague was also spread by fleas from infected rats. As a result, it always entered a town in the end. In one or two Italian towns the first victims of plague were boarded up inside their houses to die and rot along with their families. Within each family the healthy members avoided the dying until they caught the disease themselves. One man wrote:

> 'The sick are served as dogs would be. Food is put near the sufferer's bed and then his kinsfolk run away.'

Few doctors dared to treat the victims. Those who did so were often seized by the plague themselves. In many towns the plague killed up to half the inhabitants. Streets and doorsteps were littered with bodies every day, and, according to Boccaccio, beggars were given small sums of money to take the dead to burial pits outside the town walls.

---

1. What is quarantine? Try to find out how the word originated.

---

2. Why was quarantine of little value in preventing the spread of plague to new cities?

Posies and dung

Some people said that the plague was due to poisonous air and they tried to avoid it by holding scented flowers to their noses. Doctors who stayed in the cities put on gowns and hoods before making their calls. The hood had a sort of beak that was stuffed with herbs, or with sponges soaked in vinegar. Other people kept their heads over buckets of dung. Perhaps they thought that the evil smell would somehow defeat the poison in the atmosphere. The Pope spent most of his time between two gigantic bonfires.

Some doctors wore special hoods and gowns when they visited plague victims. They stuffed the beak with sweet-smelling herbs.

Once a person had the plague there was little anyone could do. Some doctors cut the swellings open to let out all the blood and pus; other doctors recommended applying dung (if people were poor) or mysterious mixtures (if people were rich).

---

3. List some of the things people did
(a) to escape the plague
(b) to deal with it.

---

4. The Pope did not catch plague. Suggest one or two ways in which his use of bonfires might have helped him survive.

---

5. List about five correct or nearly-correct ideas which some people had about illness and medicine during the plague.

Lack of medical progress

The Black Death came to an end in 1350. No one is sure of the reason for this. However, we know that rats often caught the disease themselves. Their numbers fell, so human beings were less at risk from their fleas and germs. Doctors had done very little to help. Some may have given advice and treatment that saved a few patients, but other doctors did more harm than good. Doctors did not even learn from the plague. Learning often depends on experiment and observation. Galen and others had already tried to learn in this scientific way, but the methods of science were not developed and widely used until later centuries. (We shall see this in the following chapters.)

Conditions were too chaotic for doctors to learn from the plague. If a doctor tried to learn about the disease by observing plague victims, it would simply increase his chances of dying. In any case, the complex links between rats, fleas, germs and humans could not be understood without two important aids. One was printing, which (from the 15th century) enabled people to share their knowledge. The other was the microscope, but this was not invented until the 17th century.

The plague showed the link between dirt and disease, but cities remained a breeding ground for infection and vermin. As a result, there were several further outbreaks of plague. The most famous epidemic in Britain occurred in 1666. The most recent outbreak occurred about 80 years ago, killing 25 people in parts of Suffolk. The disease is still found in many poor countries and could spread to Europe again in the future.

---

6. List some of the factors that hindered medical progress during the 14th century.

Chapter 11 Anatomy in the Renaissance

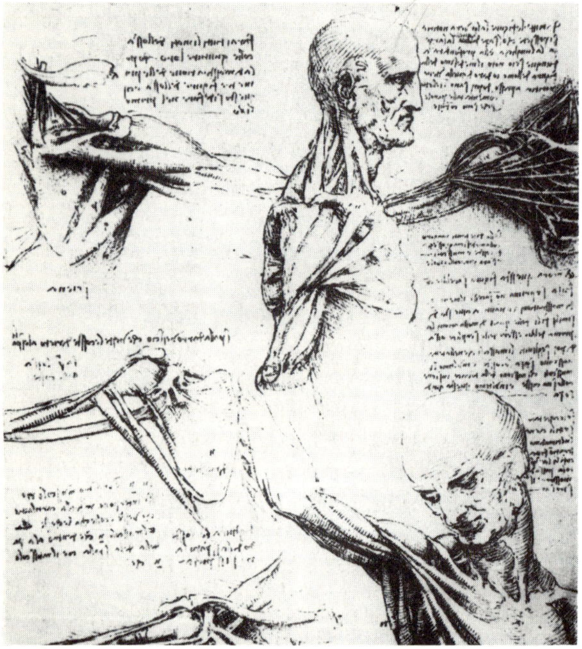

Leonardo da Vinci did not believe everything he read! He studied human corpses himself and made accurate drawings like the ones above.

The Renaissance was a period which began at the end of the 14th century. Before this time the Church and the State had a strong influence over what people thought and did. They tried to control people's thoughts by punishing those who dared to write or say things with which they disagreed. Religious, medical and other writings had to fit in with what the Church taught.

In the Renaissance the Church's control of thought became a little weaker. This occurred for various reasons. One was the discovery of America, which showed the value of finding things out instead of sticking to old ideas. More important was the invention of printing, which made it hard for the Church to prevent the rapid spread of new ideas. Printing meant that scholars could read more works by the ancient Greeks and Romans, including plays and philosophical writings. These writings did not contain Christian ideas about man and God. Some described pagans who faced problems bravely, even though they were doomed to fail. To people who read these works in the 15th and 16th centuries, human life began to seem exciting and challenging.

The Church had always encouraged people to feel a sense of shame about themselves and their bodies. This feeling continued so far as poorer people (and especially women) were concerned. However, many Renaissance men gained a new sense of dignity and independence. Inspired by Greek statues, they tried to express the noble side of human nature in works of art. The greatest Renaissance artists were the Italians Leonardo da Vinci and Michelangelo, who worked in the late 15th and early 16th centuries. They felt that the body was beautiful, but they also admired its strength and construction. To understand its muscles and the way they worked they studied anatomy for themselves. So fine and exact were their drawings and paintings that surgeons sometimes studied them before beginning operations.

1. The Renaissance was a time when men discovered new ways of thinking. How did printing help in this?

2. How did Leonardo da Vinci and Michelangelo help the progress of medicine? Why did they do it?

Vesalius showing the muscles of the human arm.

Vesalius

Vesalius was a Flemish anatomist who lived in the 16th century. After carrying out many human dissections Vesalius corrected the false ideas of Galen and Mondino. For example, he said that no blood can pass through the central muscle of the heart.

He also disproved the traditional view that women have more ribs than men. In showing that both sexes have the same number, Vesalius angered the Church authorities. This was because they believed that God had taken a rib from the first man, Adam, and used it to make the first woman, Eve. In the end they forced Vesalius to give up his work. However, printed copies of his textbook *On the Fabric of the Human Body* were used by students instead of books by Mondino and Galen. The Church could no longer put a stop to dissections and these were performed in front of students while passages from Vesalius' work were read aloud.

The title page of Vesalius' famous textbook.

Paré

The introduction of gunpowder in the 14th century had a major influence on the progress of medicine. This was because the use of gunpowder increased the number of wounded soldiers. This in turn increased the demand for army surgeons and led to the revolutionary work of a French army surgeon called Ambrosius Paré (1510–1590). He disagreed with the practice of pouring boiling oil over gunshot wounds. Perhaps this was done to prevent wounds from going bad and festering. If so, it showed that the ideas of medieval doctors like de Luccas and Henri de Mondeville were being accepted. However, the oil caused burns and pain which hindered the soldiers' recovery. Paré obtained much better results by using a mixture of egg and cold oils. He taught other surgeons how wrong it was to interfere with nature too much, and this brought a big improvement in the way injured people were treated.

---

3. The first accurate anatomical drawings were made in the Renaissance. Why do you think this was?

---

4. Which false ideas did Vesalius contradict? Use your own words to explain how this got him into trouble.

---

5. How did the introduction of gunpowder help the progress of medicine?

---

6. How were gunshot wounds treated when Paré began work? How did Paré treat them? What did he learn from his success?

Conclusion

Vesalius corrected many mistakes made by Galen and others. Moreover, in learning about the human body by careful dissection he and the Italian artists encouraged a new approach to learning. What mattered to them, and to Paré too, was observation. In this way they were setting an example of careful scientific work.

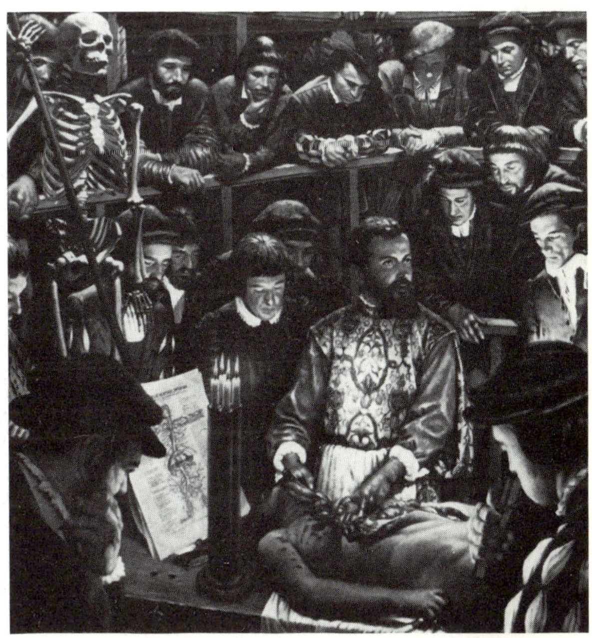

Vesalius dissecting a body in front of some medical students.

Chapter 12 Medicine in the 17th and 18th centuries

William Harvey explaining the working of the heart to King Charles I.

In the 17th and 18th centuries people continued to think and discover for themselves. They began to find new clues about the movement of blood inside the body. For example, they found that valves control the direction of blood in the veins and arteries. The veins take blood **towards** the heart and the arteries carry it **away from** the heart. The new discoveries contradicted Galen's idea of an ebb and flow within the blood-vessels.

The man who found out most about the movement of blood was William Harvey, who did his work in the early part of the 17th century. Harvey carried out experiments to check how the valves in blood vessels worked. For example, he emptied a vein in his arm by pressing his finger along the vein towards the wrist. Blood from the upper part of his arm did not run backwards and fill up the vein since the valves in the vein prevented this. However, the vein refilled when he took his finger away and allowed blood to flow in the proper direction.

Harvey decided to work out the weight of blood which left his heart in an hour. He found that it came to three times the weight of his body. This disproved the old idea that blood was used up and replaced from food, for a person would have to eat three times the weight of his body every hour of his life. No one could ever eat so much, not even for a single hour. Harvey realised that the same blood must circulate round the lungs and the body time and again.

There was one point which Harvey could not check. He knew that arteries branched repeatedly, getting smaller and smaller until the tiniest ones were hardly visible. He also knew that the smallest veins joined together to form the giant ones which enter the heart. However, he could not see any minute vessels linking the smallest arteries and the smallest veins. Without them the circulatory system would not be complete. Although he had no way of seeing them, Harvey was sure these vessels existed.

New tools and instruments

Curiosity often led people to make new tools and instruments. At the start of the 17th century an Italian called Santorio built a weighing machine which was large enough to hold himself and a table and chair. He spent weeks on the machine, studying the changes in his weight which resulted from functions like digestion and sweating. He also invented a thermometer for checking a person's temperature. This became an important aid in diagnosing illnesses.

In 1609 the Dutch spectacle-maker, Jansen, used two lenses to make a simple microscope. Later in the century, other people made micro-

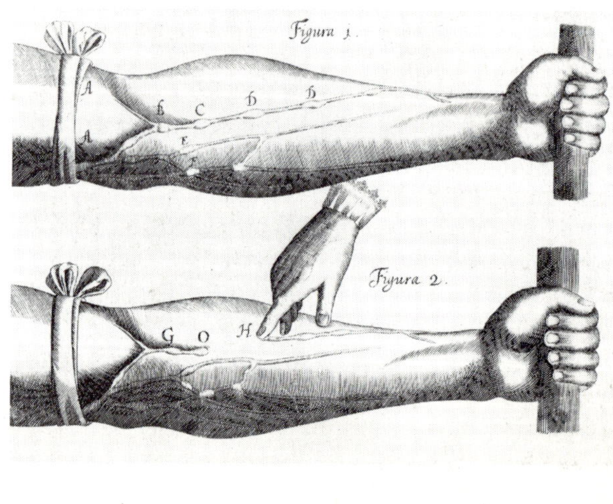

These drawings appeared in a book by Harvey. They helped to explain how the valves in a person's blood-vessels work.

scopes with greater magnifying power. These were used for important work in medicine and biology. Marcello Malpighi, an Italian anatomist, found that Harvey's ideas were correct, for he saw the minute blood-vessels (called *capillaries*) which link the arteries with the veins.

The Dutchman, van Leeuwenhoek, used microscopes to look at his skin, his spit and the dirt on his teeth. He found to his amazement that they were teeming with tiny organisms. (We usually called them *microbes* or *bacteria*, but the ones that can do us harm are sometimes referred to as germs.) Other scientists studied blood, and they found that the liquid (called *plasma*) was full of tiny cells (called corpuscles), which carry oxygen from the lungs to the rest of the body.

1. In your own words, write about two of the experiments described above. Name the scientist involved and say what he learned from the experiment.

2. Look at the drawings from Harvey's book and describe what is happening in the lower one.

3. What are capillaries? What made Harvey sure that they existed? Why was it left to someone else to prove their existence?

Edward Jenner and vaccination

People continued to learn by experiment and observation. In the second half of the 18th century an English country doctor called Edward Jenner

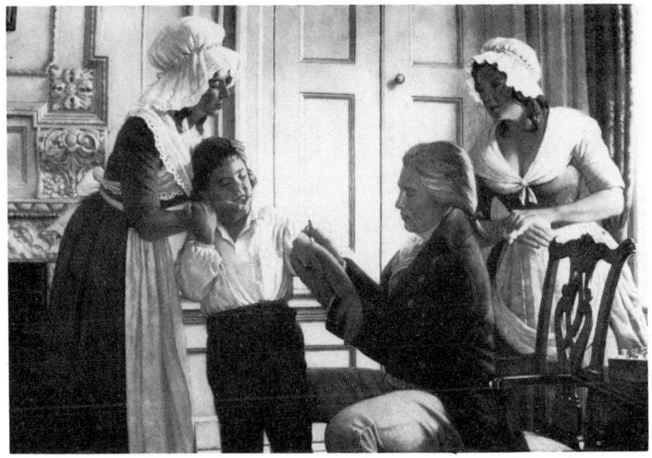

Edward Jenner and James Phipps.

studied the link between cowpox and smallpox. Cowpox was a mild disease which affected the teats of cows. It also affected milkmaids' hands and it gave them sores on other parts of their bodies too. Milkmaids were glad to get cowpox, since it seemed to stop them from getting smallpox later on. They knew that smallpox could kill them or leave them with terrible scars.

Jenner decided to try an experiment. He took a healthy boy, James Phipps, and gave him a dose of cowpox germs through two small cuts in one of his arms. Six weeks later he gave the boy some smallpox germs 'but no disease followed'.

Jenner had found that injecting people with cowpox germs protected them from smallpox. This type of treatment soon became known as *vaccination* (from the Latin for cow). Its worldwide use means that smallpox is almost unknown today. Jenner did not understand how his vaccination worked but scientists in the 19th century found this out (see Chapter 18).

4. In the 18th century, milkmaids were sometimes called 'pretty maids'. How was this connected with cowpox?

5. How might Jenner have explained his experiment to the boy? What do you think the boy's feelings were?

6. Why is smallpox so rare today?

Some people published this cartoon when they heard of the work which Jenner was doing. What attitude did these people have? Why do you think they felt like this?

Chapter 13 Spontaneous generation and the work of Pasteur

Since the earliest times, many people throughout the world had believed in *spontaneous generation.* This was the idea that living things could appear as if by magic if conditions were right. For example, they believed that crocodiles came to life by themselves in the muddy banks of the River Nile, and that rotting meat simply turned into maggots. They had no idea that crocodiles came from the eggs of other crocodiles, or that maggots came from the eggs of flies.

For mice to appear, all that seemed to be needed was the sacking, flour and dust on the floor of a baker's shop. When a few 18th-century scientists questioned the truth of spontaneous generation people tried to defend the theory in various ways. Some of them wrote out recipes for creating mice with just the right amounts of sacking and other ingredients. When the recipes were tried mice often appeared. As a result of cases like this, most people felt that the theory was proved.

Scientists using microscopes discovered germs in the blood of sick people. However, they did not realise that the germs had made the people ill. Instead, they thought the diseases had somehow caused the germs. It seemed to them that a sick person's blood was a place where germs came into existence, just as the mud of the River Nile was a source of living crocodiles. Germs has been found, but the cause of diseases was still not properly understood.

1. Explain the idea of spontaneous generation in your own words. What four examples of spontaneous generation are mentioned above?

2. How did people try to prove that spontaneous generation was true? Why do you think their experiments appeared to work?

3. What did 18th-century scientists find in the blood of people with infectious diseases? In what two ways could this be explained?

Louis Pasteur

Louis Pasteur was a French chemist who lived in the 19th century. He was convinced that spontaneous generation did not occur, and he carried out experiments to prove that he was right. For one experiment he used some liquid which normally went bad quickly when exposed to the air. He also used two glass containers with very long spouts. (Apart from the spouts, they could both be sealed to keep out germs.) Pasteur put some liquid in each container and boiled it to kill all the germs that were present. He also heated the spout of one container until it started to melt; then he bent it into a curvy shape.

Pasteur said the liquid in this container would last for years, since the bend in the spout would slow down any movement of air. The germs in the air would settle in the lowest part of the curve and

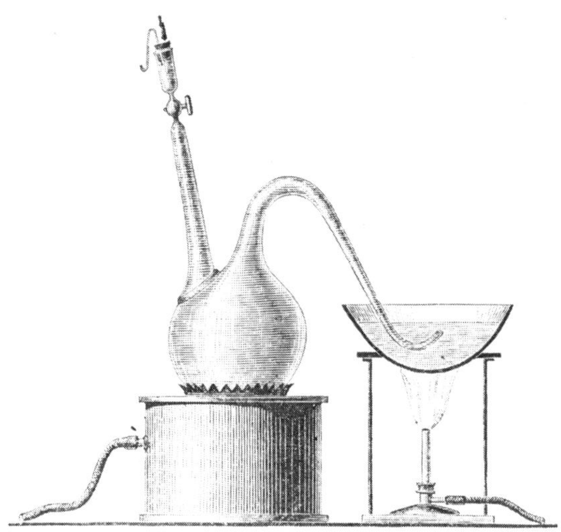

One of the flasks used by Louis Pasteur in his famous experiment. The neck has been bent and heat is now being used to kill germs.

would not reach the liquid. The straight spout on the other container would let in germs more easily, and the liquid there would soon go bad.

Everything Pasteur said was correct. His experiment proved that germs did not come alive by themselves; they would only be found in places they were able to reach.

Pasteur's advice

In 1850, Pasteur said,

> 'If I were a surgeon, impressed as I am with the dangers to which the patient is exposed by microbes

present over the surface of all objects, particularly in hospitals, not only would I use none but perfectly clean instruments, but after having cleansed my hands with the greatest care, and subjected them to a rapid flaming ... I would use only lint, bandages and sponges previously exposed to a temperature of 130° to 150°C.'

As we shall see, nearly all this advice was followed, but not for many years.

---

4. Make two labelled drawings to show how Pasteur's experiment worked. Use the illustration to help you but remember that one container should be slightly different.

---

5. Pasteur said that shaking the container with the bent spout would lead to the liquid going bad. Why do think this would happen?

---

6. What was the point of Pasteur's advice in 1850?

Making new vaccines

Pasteur was asked to deal with diseases affecting animals. He quickly found that germs were the cause, and he guessed that the answer might be the use of new vaccinations. No one was sure how Jenner's vaccine protected human beings from smallpox, so developing vaccines for animals was very hard. In the end Pasteur found the answer by chance. He was working on a poultry disease called chicken cholera. He needed chickens that had the disease so he sometimes gave them injections of germs. One day Pasteur's assistant used a batch of germs that were old and weak, and to Pasteur's surprise nothing happened at all. The chickens stayed healthy even after a further injection with stronger germs.

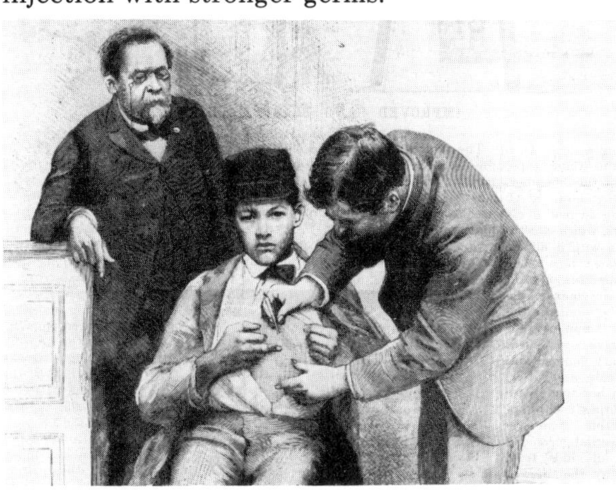

Pasteur watches as his assistant tests the rabies vaccine on a human being for the first time.

A vaccine for rabies

By using old or heat-weakened germs Pasteur soon developed vaccines not only for chicken cholera but also for anthrax, a cattle disease.

Pasteur felt sure that vaccines could be developed to deal with many diseases affecting humans. One disease he studied was rabies. This disease causes madness and death in dogs – and it does the same to humans if an infected dog bites them. To make a new vaccine Pasteur infected rabbits with rabies. After their death he took out their spinal cords, which were very badly affected. He dried the cords and saved them for a fortnight until the germs were weak. He found that solutions of this material could then be used to vaccinate dogs and other animals.

Pasteur was afraid to try out the rabies vaccine on humans. He thought that it might cause infection and death. However, one day someone brought him a boy who had been bitten by an infected dog. If nothing was done the boy would develop rabies and die so Pasteur decided to give him the vaccine. The boy remained well and Pasteur knew that his rabies vaccine had been a success. Pasteur was now rather old and ill, but other people took over the work which he had begun. Some, such as Robert Koch, identified various germs with the aid of microscopes. Other scientists found new medicines to deal with these germs. We shall look at their work in Chapter 18.

---

7. How did Pasteur make his vaccines? In what way was Jenner's vaccine similar?

A modern pasteurisation plant, where milk is heated to kill germs. The process is named after Louis Pasteur, who suggested its use.

Chapter 14 Disease in the slums

A home in a cellar.

Many towns and cities grew extremely fast in the first 50 years of the 19th century. At the start of the century Bradford had 13 000 people; by 1850 the number had risen to 104 000. People flocked to centres like Bradford for various reasons. For example, changes in farming and manufacturing forced many country families to seek new jobs. Up to this time, a lot of these families had earned their living by spinning and weaving with simple machines in country workshops and cottages. Now, however, factory owners started using steam-powered machinery to manufacture textiles. People using the older methods could not compete with factories using these new machines, which turned out cloth far more quickly and cheaply than they could.

A single factory might employ many hundreds of people. Rows of houses were built nearby for the workers to live in, and they quickly filled with people from the countryside. Sometimes this was the start of a new (but filthy and overcrowded) town. Usually, though, an existing town or city grew to many times its former size.

The factory owners paid very low wages. As a result, the workers were poor, and they had to live in very small houses. Some of the houses only had two rooms, one on each floor. A family of six or seven people would have to sleep together in the upstairs room, though there might not be sufficient space for separate beds.

> 'In Bury, the population of which was 20 000, the dwellings of 3000 families of working men were visited [by government inspectors]. In 773 of them the families slept three and four in a bed; in 209, four and five slept in a bed; in 67 five and six slept in a bed; and in 15 six and seven slept in a bed.
>
> [In Liverpool] there were 7 860 cellars ... which were dark, damp, confined, ill-ventilated and dirty. 39 000 people [had to live in these cellars].'
>
> *(From a Parliamentary Debate)*

Epidemics of cholera

Workers' houses were built 'back-to-back' to squeeze as many people as possible into each street. There were often no toilets, and people had to pour their slops into gutters outside. If the gutters became blocked the filth spread everywhere; often it oozed into rivers and wells, polluting the water which people drank.

The houses in this Glasgow alley were better than most.

What do you think the artist meant when he drew this cartoon?

The filthy, overcrowded conditions encouraged the outbreak and spread of diseases like smallpox, diphtheria, typhus and typhoid. Another disease, called cholera, broke out a number of times in the 19th century. The most serious outbreak occurred in 1832. Some people think it began in Hull, where rags were imported from European hospitals to be used in the manufacture of paper. The disease was soon killing hundreds of people in all the big slums. It easily spread within families sharing a single bedroom. Moreover, a major symptom of cholera was diarrhoea, and the use of open sewers meant that slops could quickly spread the disease from house to house and from street to street.

In some crowded areas, half the children died of diseases before they were five. However, wealthy people often chose to ignore these facts. Their own homes were spacious, clean and comfortable, and they rarely died from the diseases that killed so many people in the slums. Helping the poor would have been expensive. It would have meant higher rates and taxes for those who were rich.

---

1. Give as many reasons as you can why it was so easy for disease to spread in large cities in the 19th century.

---

2. Why did some people think that the outbreak of cholera in 1832 began in Hull? Why would this not happen today?

Children at work

Children had to work like their parents, often for over 12 hours a day, and many were injured by the machines. A man called Lord Ashley (later the Earl of Shaftesbury) spoke of the crippled children he saw in Bradford:

> 'They might be numbered by hundreds, perhaps by thousands ... They seemed to me, such were their crooked shapes, like a mass of crooked alphabets [letters].'

Lord Ashley thought it was wrong that children should suffer like this. Some were forced to work in mines, and Ashley felt that this must stop. In the end he persuaded Parliament to limit the number of hours which children had to work, and to stop them being sent down mines until they were ten.

Ashley's efforts were very important, but diseases linked to living conditions were the principal causes of death and disablement. In the following chapter we shall see how the problems of hygiene were solved.

---

3. What were the advantages of employing children in the mines and factories? What effects did this have on their health?

---

4. Why were workers (and other poor people) so badly neglected? (You may have several ideas about this.)

Children at work in a Lancashire coal-mine.

Chapter 15 Public health and the law in the 19th century

Sir Edwin Chadwick.

Edwin Chadwick was a civil servant who did his best to help the poor in the 19th century. In 1842 he prepared a report on the health and welfare of British people. It showed that the length of people's lives was greatly affected by where they lived. People living in the centre of Manchester had an average life span of only 17 years. Richer people with homes on the outskirts of Manchester lived more than twice as long. Their average life span was 38 years. In Rutland (a rural district which is now part of Leicestershire) even the poorest people lived for an average of 38 years. This was because the region did not have industrial towns. The rich folk in Rutland could afford better diets and medical care so their average life span was higher still – 52 years.

Chadwick used facts and figures like these to press for improvements in city slums. He told the wealthier people who lived in cities that they would benefit if they paid for improvements. He pointed out that they did not live as long as similar people in places like Rutland. That was because they occasionally caught diseases from people who lived in the slums. This was hardly surprising, for factory owners could not always keep away from their workers, and poor people sometimes delivered goods to the homes of the wealthy. In any case, the rich and the poor were likely to meet in streets and shops. Improving the slums would safeguard the health of the richer people, as well as the poor.

Chadwick pointed out other reasons for helping the poor. For example, the rich had to pay for the upkeep of orphans. Some of this expense would be saved if fewer parents died of disease. In addition to this, a healthier workforce would make bigger profits for those who employed them. More would be fit to turn up for work, and production levels would therefore rise.

---

1. **(a) Look at the cartoon. Do you think the family are rich or poor? How can you tell?**
   (b) The man is saying that Hampstead Heath is 'saloobrious' (healthy). What is the artist trying to say?
   (c) What was Chadwick's message to people like this?

"HAPPY HAMPSTEAD!"

(A SUBURBAN PLAY(GUE) GROUND.)

SUNDAY-OUTER. "HA, MY DEAR! NOW THIS IS WHAT I CALL PLEASANT AND SALOOBRIOUS! DO THE YOUNG 'UNS NO END O' GOOD. LET'S GET ON TO THE 'EATH."

A cartoon from the magazine Punch *(1875).*

The first Public Health Act

Many people paid attention to Chadwick's pleas.

In 1848, the Government passed the first-ever Health Act. Under the Act, a Central Board of Health was set up to supervise Local Boards of Health in towns and cities throughout the land. These Local Boards were set up where public demand was strong; they were also set up wherever the death rate was very high. They had the power to cleanse the streets and clear away rubbish. They could also provide clean water and proper underground sewers. Since these cost a great deal of money, Local Boards were given the power to raise money by collecting rates.

The work of improving the slums began, and subsequent epidemics of cholera caused far fewer deaths than the one in 1832. This helped to prove that the work was worthwhile. Many councils were lazy, but others increased the pace at which improvements were made.

In 1855, Manchester council forbade the building of back-to-back houses. Three years later, Liverpool council appointed a Medical Officer of Health, with the job of advising on ways of making the city healthier. Public toilets were soon built in various parts of the city.

---

2. List some of the things that Local Boards of Health could do.

---

3. Why do you think public toilets were far more important in the 19th century than they are today?

Better homes were built for workers in the second half of the 19th century.

A room in a worker's house at the end of the 19th century. Compare this room with the one on page 30.

The second Public Health Act

In 1867, many poorer people were given the right to vote for MPs in general elections. This meant that their requirements and wishes carried more weight than ever before. Their biggest need was for better housing. Districts were cleaner, but very few houses had been rebuilt, and many families still lived in cellars. At last, in 1875, Parliament said that councils could buy up all the houses in a slum. They could then pull them down and build better houses in their place. The weakness in this was that councils were merely **permitted** to act; there were very few laws to **make** city councils improve housing conditions.

The turning point came when a new Public Health Act was passed towards the end of that year (1875). Under this Act, councils were forced to appoint a Medical Officer of Health and an Inspector of Nuisances. ('Nuisances' were harmful things like smoke and uncollected rubbish.) The Act included all sorts of rules about drainage, water and other matters affecting health. Councils **had** to obey these rules, though some of them did so very unwillingly.

From this time onwards, governments and councils slowly came to accept that they were responsible for public health. Thanks to improvements in hygiene and health care, the diseases which killed so many in the 19th-century slums are quite rare today in developed countries such as Great Britain.

---

4. What change in the law was made in 1867? What effect did it have?

---

5. List some of the most important points in the Act of 1875.

Chapter 16 Hospitals: places of filth and pain

Florence Nightingale.

Hospitals in Europe began in various ways. Some were started by the Church in the Middle Ages. These included hospitals such as St Bartholomew's and St Thomas's in London, which were later taken over by the civil authorities and still do excellent work today. The Church also started asylums for those with mental diseases or leprosy (which other people were frightened of catching). The civil authorities took over these hospitals too, closing some and neglecting the rest. Those which remained by the 18th century were filthy places resembling prisons. By this time there were also 'cottage hospitals' in many towns. These were started by doctors as private clinics for those who were very rich.

In the 18th century a number of hospitals were opened in cities throughout Great Britain. Most of these were 'voluntary' hospitals, funded and used by those who chose to pay a subscription every year. In those days, doctors and surgeons usually charged for each bit of treatment they gave, but the patients' subscriptions covered these charges. In certain cities, such as Leeds, subscribers could also send friends for free treatment. In spite of this, not everyone could use the new hospitals. While tradesmen could often afford to subscribe, the poor could not, and they rarely had well-off friends who would send them to hospital free of charge. New laws in the 19th century helped to solve this problem. They led to the founding of hospitals which admitted even the very poor. Sadly, however, the standards of care and cleanliness were usually low.

Filth and disease

Conditions in military hospitals were especially poor. In the 1850s a nurse called Florence Nightingale went to treat wounded soldiers in a hospital in southern Russia. She found that

> 'the wind blew [filthy] air up the pipes of open privies [toilets] into the corridors and wards'.

As a result, a lot of the patients died of infectious diseases like cholera.

Even in Britain,

> 'patients were often covered in fleas, and the bedding was hardly ever changed ... The surgeons ... with their dirty knives spread infection as well as agony and terror among the patients. Sometimes their coats were stiff with dried blood'.

One of the greatest surgeons in the 19th century, Professor von Nussbaum of Munich, admitted in 1874 that 80% of his operations led to the death of a patient. He explained that a form of infection called *gangrene* 'gnawed at every wound like an animal'. All hospital patients with open wounds faced the likelihood of being infected. The evil-smelling hospital air was full of germs, and they covered the surgeon's knife and hands even if they appeared to be clean.

At first it is hard to understand why hospital staff did not put an end to filthy conditions and unhygienic practices as quickly as possible. There were various reasons. Surgeons were proud of their old-fashioned methods: a blood-spattered gown showed that a surgeon had lots of experience! Also, Louis Pasteur's ideas about airborne germs were spreading only slowly, and many surgeons believed that he was wrong. These surgeons still clung to Galen's idea that pus must appear before wounds can heal. Lastly, of course, if people died (as most of them did), they could not complain about how they had been treated.

1. Look at the cartoon, which appeared in the middle of the 19th century. What do you think the artist was saying?

The problem of pain

In the 1840s a Scottish surgeon called James Simpson pointed out that infection was not the only reason why patients often died after operations. They also died because the terrible pain of the operation had caused a condition known as 'shock'. This affected bodily functions such as breathing and heart beat.

Good anaesthetics had not been invented, so surgeons could do very little to ease the agony cause by operations. Since ancient times they had doped their patients with drugs obtained from plants like the poppy. These helped to dull the patients' pain. In spite of this, most surgeons had to pay assistants to hold people down while they operated.

The problem of pain meant that surgeons tried to do operations as quickly as possible. Removing a limb, which might take more than two hours today, was often done in less than two minutes. Because surgeons had to work so fast they could not take proper care. A surgeon's methods were rather like those of a butcher, and patients were at risk from excessive bleeding or other complications, as well as from shock and infected wounds.

An operation at Charing Cross Hospital, London, in the second half of the 19th century.

Sudden pain causes muscles to tighten automatically. The muscular action could move the surgeon's scalpel or knife as he tried to work. This made it hard to do small and delicate operations. The need for speed meant that operations deep in the body were out of the question. Nowadays, surgeons can reach and remove an infected appendix. Without anaesthetics, doctors rarely attempted to do this, and appendicitis was usually fatal. There were also cases where patients refused operations which could have been done. They preferred to die of their illnesses rather than face the pain and risks of surgery.

2. Several types of hospital are mentioned in this chapter. Make a list of them and in each case say how treatment there was paid for.

3. Gangrene and shock were common causes of death in 18th century hospitals. What was the main cause of each?

4. Cave people had a better chance of recovering from their head operations than patients at 19th century hospitals. What do you think were the reasons for this?

Chapter 17 Hospitals: overcoming the problems

The effects of chloroform. What do you think the cartoonist's attitude might have been?

A chloroform inhaler (right).

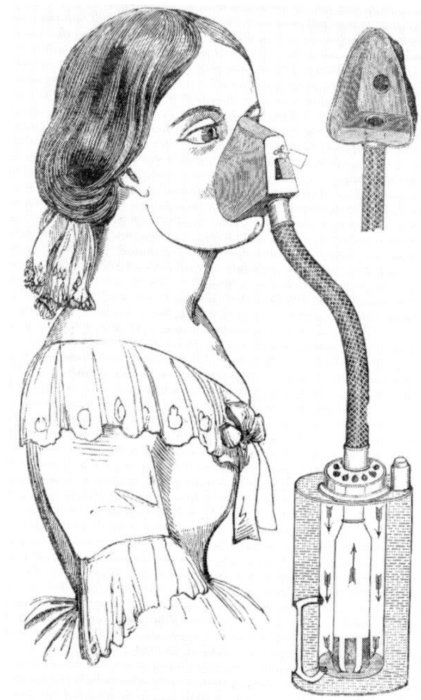

At the start of the 19th century a scientist called Sir Humphrey Davy had tried the effects of breathing a gas called nitrous oxide (laughing gas). He found that it made him light-headed and could send him to sleep if he breathed it for long. He suggested its use as an *anaesthetic*. His pupil, Michael Faraday, found that the fumes of a liquid called ether could also be used.

In the 1840s the new anaesthetics were tested by several American dentists. They found that it was hard to store and use nitrous oxide, but ether was easy to use and effective. The dentist could sprinkle some onto a cloth and put it over the patient's face. This would make him completely unconscious.

The use of ether soon became widespread. It was introduced at the General Infirmary, Leeds, in 1847. There were problems, however, for ether tended to irritate the patients' lungs. Because of this, Sir James Simpson soon introduced a new anaesthetic called chloroform. It did not hurt the patients' lungs but it worked just like ether. (The cartoon shows Simpson and some of his friends after testing chloroform on themselves.) It quickly came into general use, and was usually given by means of a simple inhaler like the one in the drawing.

Opposition to anaesthetics

Some people said that the use of anaesthetics was wrong. They were angry when doctors gave chloroform to women in labour. They pointed out a Bible verse which seemed to say that birth must be painful. Simpson queried the meaning of this particular verse. He pointed out another verse which said that God had made Adam unconscious before removing his rib to make Eve. Perhaps this meant that doctors could use anaesthetics to save men and women from pain. Queen Victoria's use of chloroform when she gave birth in 1857 did a lot to overcome people's objections.

---

1. What is an anaesthetic? Why did chloroform become the most popular anaesthetic? (There are a number of reasons.)

---

2. Which religious objection to anaesthetics did Queen Victoria help to dispel? How did she do this?

The growth of surgery

With the introduction of anaesthetics the number of surgical patients rose rapidly. For example, only 200 major operations were carried out at Leeds General Infirmary in 1862, while in 1874 the number was 649. Surgeons could now take far more time and care with their work. Because of this, most risks (including the risk of infection) were less severe than they had been before.

In the last 25 years of the 19th century surgeons learned to carry out all sorts of operations which had been difficult or impossible without anaesthetics. At Leeds, the number of operations on the stomach, intestines and ovaries rose from 15 a year to over 100. However, these long operations involved a very high risk of infection and death.

3. How did surgery change when anaesthetics were introduced? Which well-known danger did surgeons now need to concentrate on overcoming?

Joseph Lister

In 1867 a surgeon called Joseph Lister was appointed to work in the newly-built Glasgow Royal Infirmary. The authorities hoped that the clean new building would be a safe place for operations, but even here up to 50% of the patients died from infected wounds.

Lister knew that air is always full of germs, even in the cleanest conditions. There would also be many millions of germs on the patient's skin and the surgeon's hands. However, Lister had heard about an *antiseptic* (or germ-killing) substance called carbolic acid. Carbolic acid had been used successfully for cleaning sewers.

Lister decided to try carbolic acid during surgical operations. He used it to wash his hands and all his instruments before he began. More important than that, he made his assistants work a spraying machine throughout each operation. This filled the air with a very fine mist of carbolic acid, so that hardly a single germ could survive. Lister's patients survived instead! However, the use of carbolic acid did have some drawbacks. It irritated the surgeon's hands and the patient's flesh, and it failed to kill germs in grease and dirt.

At the end of the 19th century surgeons stopped using antiseptic mists. Instead, they found alternative ways of excluding infection. For example, they used boiling water or very hot steam to sterilise dressings. They also began to wear sterilised masks, gowns and rubber gloves for each operation. This ensured that the germs on their skin and in their breath did not reach the patient. Precautions like these are still in use, and modern hospitals also have air conditioning apparatus. This filters out the airborne germs before they can reach the operating theatre.

4. Lister's method was rejected, but what important idea did he try to put into practice?

5. Look again at Pasteur's advice in Chapter 13. Why do you think that Lister gets most of the credit for making surgery safer?

6. Compare the illustrations of operations in chapters 16 and 17. In each case point out the features you think are good or bad. Which development do you think was the most important? Try to give reasons.

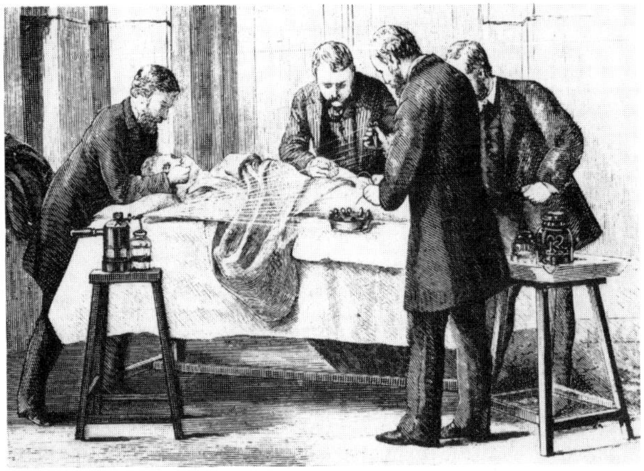

Lister's carbolic spray in use.

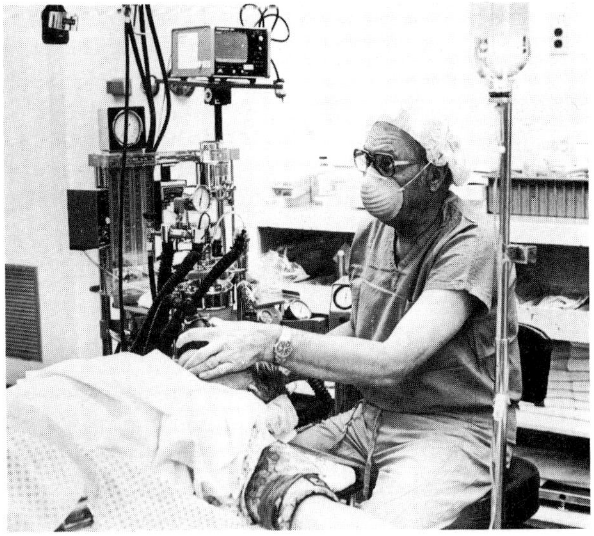

Giving an anaesthetic gas in a modern hosptial.

Chapter 18 Creating new medicines

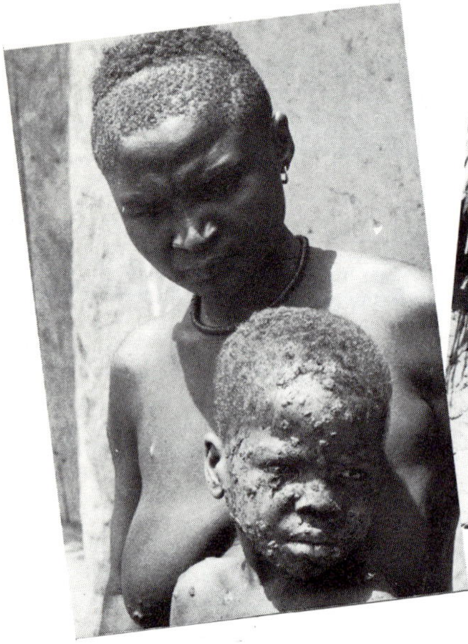

A single injection of penicillin can cure a serious disease called yaws.

As we have seen, Louis Pasteur developed various vaccines. However, he had very little idea of how they worked. A German doctor called Emil Behring discovered the answer to this in the 1880s. He explained that when someone overcomes infection (or the weakened germs in a dose of vaccine) his body produces special cells (called *antibodies*) that can deal with similar germs again. This understanding enabled Behring to continue the fight against diseases. One of his most important achievements came after he had infected animals with diphtheria. Some of the animals recovered, and Behring took samples of their blood. He found that the fluid part of their blood contained diphtheria antibodies. He also found that preparations of this could be used as a special medicine (or *serum*) to cure the disease in human beings.

A Japanese scientist, Kitasato, did similar work with the germ that caused tetanus. He too produced a useful serum, and in 1890 he and Behring published an essay announcing their findings.

'Magic bullets'

Serums were developed for several diseases, but other diseases could not be treated in this way. It seemed that they could never be treated, for germ-killing substances made by man attacked human tissue as well as germs. This was the case with carbolic acid. If injected into the patient's body or given by mouth it would poison and kill him. A German scientist called Paul Ehrlich dreamed of creating a '*magic bullet*' – a substance which would pick out and kill the germs that were making a person ill, while leaving his tissues completely unharmed.

Ehrlich and his assistants tried to create a 'magic bullet' to cure a disease called syphilis. The task appeared impossible, for they made and tested 600 different preparations without success. However, their 606th preparation worked quite well. They called the substance '606' or Salvarsan. This was produced in 1910, and other scientists soon produced 'magic bullets' for curing other diseases. For example, a family of drugs called *sulphonamides* were introduced in the 1930s to cure diseases such as pneumonia.

---

1. Carbolic acid was a powerful germ-killer. Why could it not be used to cure infectious diseases?

---

2. Ehrlich said he wanted to find a 'magic bullet'. What did he mean?

Penicillin

There were still many germs that could not be killed, even with sulphonamides. For example, there was no reliable way of killing the germs that often infected wounds. World War 1, which ended in 1918, had helped to make people aware of this problem, for thousands of soldiers died after minor wounds became septic. A Scottish doctor called Alexander Fleming had seen this happen in hundreds of cases, and he made up his mind to stop these deaths from occurring in future.

After the war, Fleming worked in a hospital laboratory where he studied the sort of germs that had caused the battlefield deaths (and sometimes killed people who had operations). Fleming allowed his samples of germs to multiply in small glass dishes containing a jelly-like substance called agar. The germs spread over the surface of this agar. One day Fleming found that some mould was growing in one of the dishes and was killing the germs. He also found that preparations made from this mould killed most sorts of germs in the human body. This was the basis of a new drug known as *penicillin*. By the end of 1945 it had saved the lives of thousands of soldiers in World War 2.

Nowadays, penicillin and other similar drugs are mass-produced. They are generally known as *antibiotics*, and are used in the treatment of many complaints. For example, children's ear infections are usually cured with antibiotics.

---

3. How was the discovery of penicillin hastened
(a) by war, and
(b) by luck?

---

4. Look again at Chapter 9. Which form of treatment could have given Fleming a useful clue?

---

5. List the main drugs described in this chapter. State the approximate dates when they were introduced and give an example of the sort of disease each drug could fight.

Fleming at work in his laboratory.

Chapter 19 Holistic medicine and positive health

GUIDE TO HEALTHY MEALS

We asked some people what sort of meals and snacks they ate regularly, and asked a nutritionist to give a verdict on each meal and suggest ways of making small changes to improve them.

Breakfast ...

Bowl of unsugared muesli, cup of coffee. Both with semi-skimmed milk.
Very good choice.

Bowl of cornflakes with sugar and ordinary milk.
You could improve this by using a low fat milk and less sugar. And you could increase the fibre content by choosing a wholewheat cereal rather than cornflakes.

Toast and marmalade. Cup of tea with sugar.
Using wholemeal bread for the toast would provide much more fibre. Try cutting down the sugar in your tea. This is particularly easy when you're drinking it with a sweet food like marmalade.

Snacks & Packed Lunches ...

Baked beans on toast
Good choice, especially if you buy the beans with less sugar and salt. Go for wholemeal toast. You won't need much, if any, butter or margarine on the toast.

Exercise is good for us all – so is healthy diet.

We have seen the success of doctors and medical scientists in creating 'magic bullets' to deal with infectious diseases. In the last fifty years, more and more drugs and medicines have been introduced to deal with other conditions. However, there are dangers in thinking of illnesses as particular targets, each of which can be reached and destroyed with the right sort of pill. For one thing, we tend to ignore the question of why an illness occurs in the first place.

The natural world is a complex system of cause and effect. For example, within a living body each organ depends on the action of all the other organs. In turn, the overall health of the body depends on the person's state of mind, environment, diet and way of life.

Many conditions can be eased or cured by the use of drugs. However, a problem may well return – or be replaced by a different one – unless the cause is found and remedied. For example, indigestion can often be eased by taking stomach pills. However, if the cause is too much worry and stress in the person's life, he or she may quickly develop sleeplessness or some other problem. Facts like these help to show the importance of treating the patient 'as a whole'. This means taking full account of his circumstances, way of life and general health. Medicine which aims to do this is called *holistic medicine.*

1. What is holistic medicine? In what ways is it different from other approaches to healing?

The power of advertisements

Holistic medicine is nothing new. Its neglect in the developed countries during the present century has various causes. One has been the effectiveness of some 'magic bullets'. This has led to people trusting drugs too much. Advertising has done a lot to increase their use. Advertisements often show headache and indigestion remedies 'homing in' on the part that hurts and solving the problem almost instantly. Patients have learned to expect a quick, direct form of treatment for all their complaints, and doctors often lack the time and the training to look very deeply into each case.

Holistic medicine and politics

Holistic answers are not always easy. For example, excessive noise can cause headaches, and can also damage a person's hearing. It is clear that tablets are not the best answer for headaches which are caused like this. However, excessive noise at work may need to be dealt with by trades unions or politicians. In practice, the patient may have to take tablets after all.

Unemployment, poverty, boredom, bad housing and family problems can cause or worsen anxiety, depression and sleeplessness. They can also lead to physical illness. Sleeping pills and other drugs may help some people to cope for a while but the ideal answers may again be social or political.

2. Why are holistic answers often hard to apply? What do people do instead?

Side effects

Drugs can often have side effects. In the 1960s a drug called thalidomide was given to pregnant women as a sedative. In many cases it caused their babies to be born with deformities. Few drugs have done as much harm as that. However, as many as 10% of hospital patients in western countries are there to be treated for the after-effects of medical drugs.

Most people suffer from side effects at some time or other. Drowsiness is one of the commonest side effects of many drugs, and this can lead to accidents if people drive or work machinery. Other drugs cause stomach upsets and diarrhoea. Few are exact and limited in their effects, and terms like 'magic bullet' are really too optimistic. Even worse, new strains of germs are becoming resistant to drugs based on penicillin. As a result, these drugs are becoming less effective.

3. List some disadvantages in depending on modern drugs too much.

Positive health

Nowadays there is a growing concern with positive health and the prevention of illness. People are learning that exercise is very important. They are also learning to eat a good diet, avoiding sugary, fatty foods that can lead to overweight and disease. They know that tobacco and other addictive drugs can ruin their health.

In developed countries, immunisation gives more and more people protection from many infectious diseases. There is also an increase in *screening* procedures. Screening means checking large numbers of people who seem to be healthy. The purpose of this is to pick out for treatment those people who may have the early signs of a serious illness like lung cancer.

During this century the governments of most developed countries have realised that health is of national importance. They have organised medical services on a national basis, and the costs are met through taxes or compulsory insurance payments. As a result, there is usually nothing to pay when treatment or advice is sought. This is a very great help to the poor. It also means that facilities such as screening can be introduced as widely and cheaply as possible.

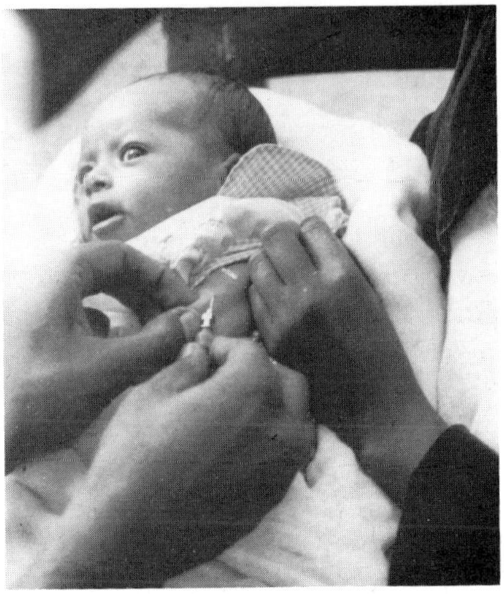

Mass vaccination prevents epidemics of fatal diseases like whooping cough.

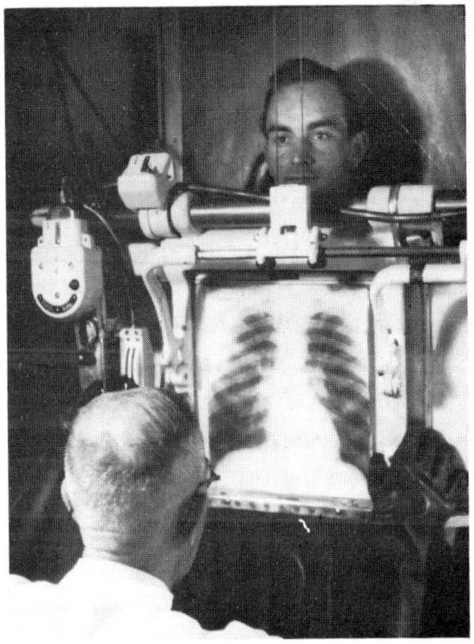

In the 20th century doctors have learned to use X-rays to see inside the body. In this way they can check large numbers of people for signs of lung disease.

4. List some of the things that are done in schools to check or safeguard pupils' health. What other things are done to safeguard the health of adults or people in general?

Chapter 20 Alternative medicine

We have already seen that people's minds affect their bodies in various ways. Treatment with drugs depends on this to some extent. Experiments have shown that pills made of sugar may do us good if we think they contain a drug we need. In a similar way, a patient's faith and confidence often add to the value of genuine medicine. A doctor may give him some sleeping pills and tell him that they are very effective. The doctor's words will increase the patient's faith in the pills. Because of this, he will go to bed in the right frame of mind, ready to have a good night's sleep.

In primitive cultures the sick person goes to the medicine man. He has learned to trust the medicine man's skill and the potions he uses. Strange rituals may increase this faith and help to bring about a cure. As we have seen, healers in other cultures have also used faith and ritual. Even today, a doctor's success may depend on having the patient's trust. Going to the doctor is part of a healing ritual, and we may be impressed by the doctor's skill and mysterious methods. We expect to be cured, and a bottle of medicine helps to keep this faith alive until the illness has gone.

Even with serious physical illness, a patient's mind may have more effect than the drugs he or she receives. Some people think that cancer patients can sometimes make themselves better by willpower.

---

1. *Placebos* are dummy pills which contain no proper medicine, and doctors sometimes talk about *the placebo effect*. What do you think they mean by this?

---

2. *Placebo* is a Latin word. Doctors used to write prescriptions in Latin, and doctors and pharmacists (chemists) still use Latin phrases. How might this affect the patient?

Faith healing

Some sick people distrust modern medicine. Perhaps it has failed to make them well, or perhaps they feel that the healing powers of the mind and the body need more stimulation. Some of these people try old-fashioned herbal remedies, while others attend public faith-healing sessions. A faith healer usually lays his hands on the patient's head or on the part of his body which is giving him trouble. Other people present may pray that the healing will be a success. Sick people sometimes feel lonely and worthless, but faith-healing sessions give them the central place in a group. The sessions may also convince them that God is going to heal them. These things increase their sense of well-being and sometimes give them the strength to recover. Whatever we think about 'miracle cures', there is little doubt that faith-healing sessions can do people good.

A faith healer at work.

Homoeopathy

Treatment by unconventional means is sometimes known as *alternative medicine*. *Homoeopathy* is one of the best-known examples. It was introduced 180 years ago by a German doctor called Samual Hahnemann. Hahnemann was shocked by the huge and sometimes fatal doses of drugs which other doctors gave their patients. The doctors did not mean to kill them; they simply believed that serious illness could only be cured with drastic remedies. Hahnemann said that a patient's symptoms should first be noted carefully. Then the doctor should choose a medicine which causes similar symptoms in a healthy person. In Hahnemann's view, tiny doses of this would cure the patient by stimulating his or her natural defences. Homoeopathy is based on Hahnemann's teachings. Its popularity seems to be growing, though some people feel that the tiny doses can have no effect.

3. In what way is homoeopathy rather like vaccination?

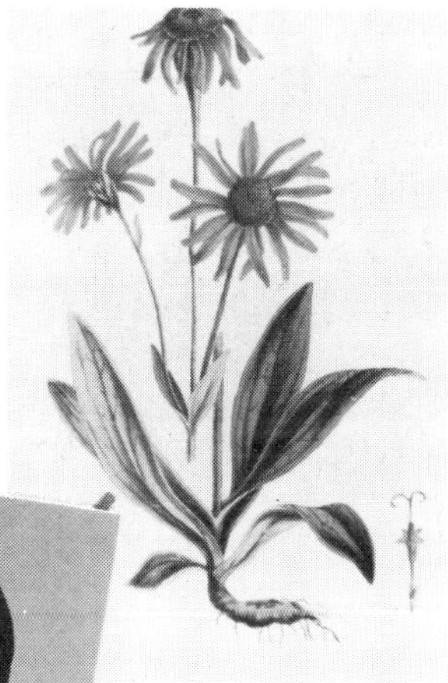

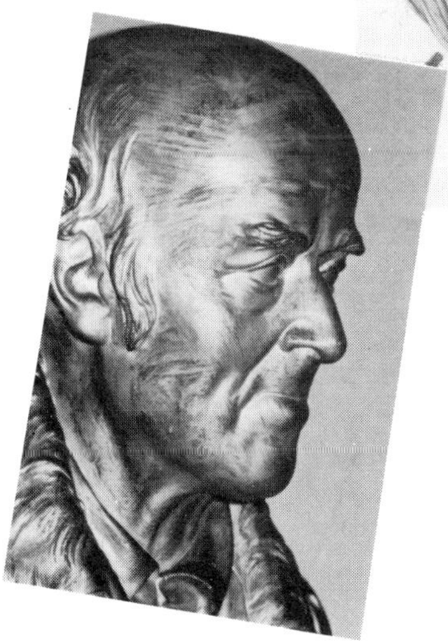

The pictures above show Hahnemann and one of the plants from which homeopathic medicines are obtained.

Acupuncture

Like homoeopathy, *acupuncture* is gaining in popularity. People in China have practised it for thousands of years and now it is being introduced into Europe and other western countries. The acupuncturist pushes the points of special needles into the patient's face or body. He chooses places thought to be linked with particular needs or illnesses. (Often these are nowhere near the site of the pain or suspected disease.) The needles are taken out again at the end of the session. Several sessions may be required, but many patients claim to be cured by this form of treatment. As with other forms of medicine, natural healing may sometimes be responsible for what occurs. However, there are reports from China that acupunture can make patients' bodies completely numb. It is said that such patients can have operations without other forms of anaesthesia. Some people think that the needles affect the patient's nerves and brain so much that his sense of pain is put out of action. Or perhaps the patient's faith in the treatment makes it work. We do not yet have a full understanding of how the mind affects our health, nor do we fully understand its part in the various forms of healing.

4. This chapter has given three examples of alternative approaches to medicine. Make notes about each. (You may want to find out more about one or two of them first.)

5. Drug companies are often hostile to alternative medicine, and so are some doctors. Suggest some possible reasons for this.

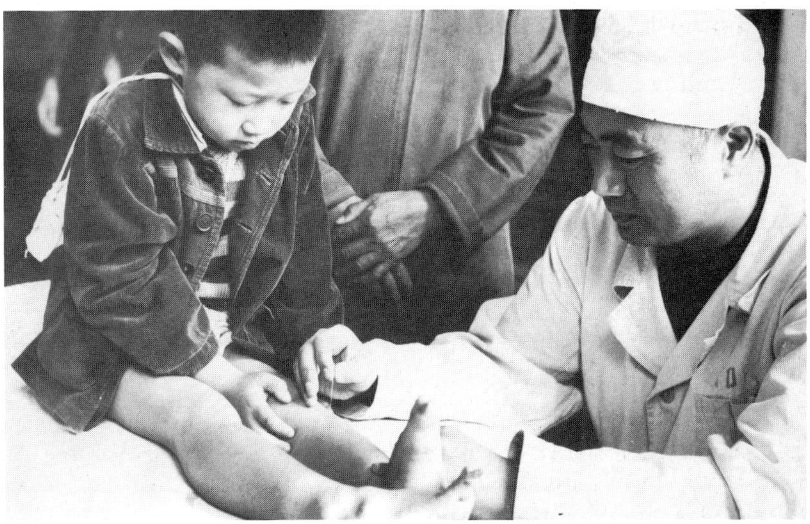

Acupuncture is being used to treat this child.

Chapter 21 Rich world and poor world

In wealthy countries such as Great Britain infectious diseases are less of a problem than ever before. This is largely due to the very high standards of public hygiene. Some infectious diseases such as colds, influenza and measles are still extremely common. However, they rarely lead to death or permanent harm.

'Rich world' diseases

In developed countries most of the serious illnesses are linked to diet, pollution and life-style. People's diets are bad because they consume too much sugar and fat, and this leads to overweight and disease. Worse still, people's diets lack fibre. This is partly because they do not eat enough fruit and vegetables. It is also because they use white flour, which lacks the outer, fibrous layer of the wheat. Appendicitis and bowel disease can often be traced to this shortage of fibre.

People in the developing world are becoming 'health conscious'.

Wealthy countries are usually highly industrialised and people depend on motor vehicles (rather than their legs) for most of their transport. All sorts of harmful chemicals come from vehicle exhausts and factory chimneys; others pour out of waste pipes into rivers and seas. Some of these substances reach people in the air they breathe; others can enter their bodies in the food they eat. Radioactive pollution can be especially dangerous, causing cancer and birth deformities.

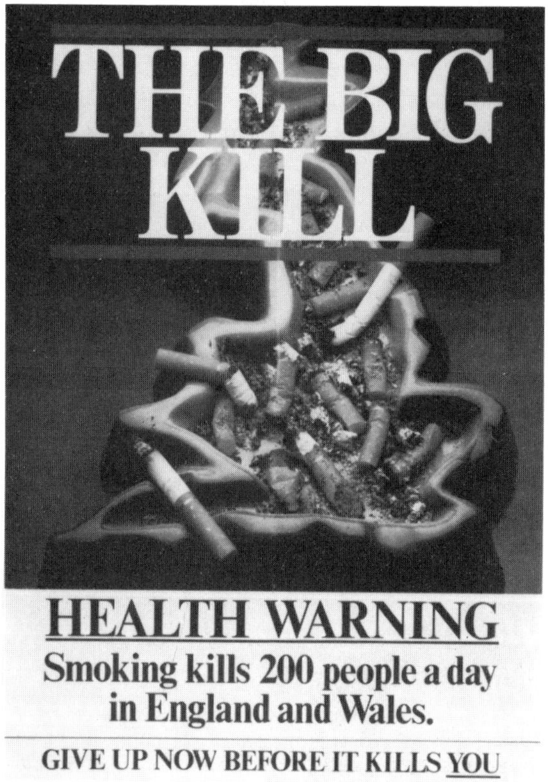

Many drugs are banned by law and the 'pushers' are punished. Why do you think tobacco can still be sold and smoked openly?

Many poisons are made for industrial purposes; others are sprayed onto crops to kill insects. In some cases small amounts of these poisons can enter and damage the human body. Chemicals which are thought to be safe for human consumption are added to many packaged foods. They preserve the food or improve its appearance, texture and taste. Some people disagree with their use, saying that they can be bad for health. Meanwhile, many millions of people make themselves ill with tobacco and alcoholic drink.

As we have seen, worry and stress can also be harmful. They often occur when people lead fast, competitive lives (as they tend to do in industrial countries). Diseases affecting the heart and blood-vessels kill roughly half the population, and most are either caused or worsened by stress, bad diet and lack of exercise.

Life expectancy

Rich world diseases most often affect the middle-aged and elderly. We need to remember this when we make comparisons, for the average life-span in wealthy countries is 70 years, while in most of the poorer developing countries it is only 30 or 40 years. Diseases connected with ageing are unlikely to occur if life-spans are short. In spite of this, there are very clear signs that diet and life-style (as well as ageing) cause rich world diseases. We can see this when people in poorer countries give up their rural way of life and move into cities. Here, the diet and way of life will be more like those in the wealthier countries. Some rich world diseases like tooth decay and appendicitis affect the young as well as the old, and when people move to the cities they soon become prone to those problems.

As for mental disease, we have already seen that societies differ in the way they treat sickness. They also differ in the way they define what sickness is. In developed countries, those who seem to act or think in unusual ways are often labelled mentally sick, and they may be kept in prisons or hospitals. In poorer countries, where families are often very large, the old and those with 'strange' ideas can be cared for and valued as part of the family.

---

1. There are many different causes of illness in developed countries. In what ways can each of the following have a bad effect on people's health:
(a) food, (b) environment and (c) work and way of life?

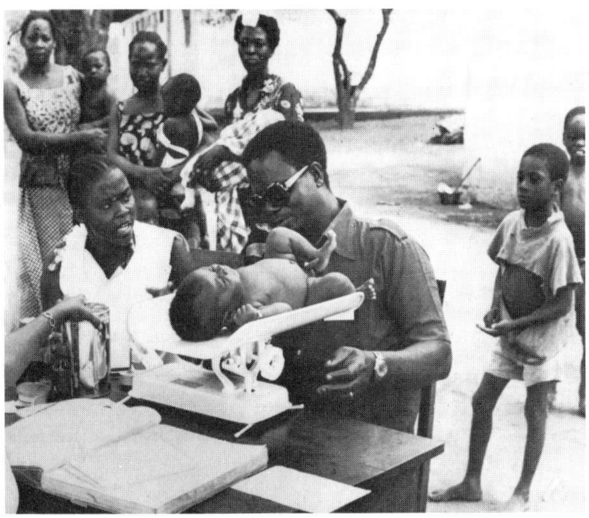

Weight and diet are often linked.

Poor diet kills adults in wealthy countries. In poorer countries it kills the young. These Indian mothers are learning which foods are best for their children.

'Third World' diseases

In poor, less developed areas, infectious disease is the main cause of death. **More than half the world's children die in this way**. The children are weakened by *malnutrition* (a scanty or poorly balanced diet) and therefore die from conditions like measles and diarrhoea, which rarely kill those with better diets. Many diseases are caught from unclean water supplies. These include a number of diarrhoeal infections; they also include conditions caused by parasites. **Unclean water is said to cause three-quarters of all the world's disease**. Third World diseases are also spread by various insects. A well-known example is the disease malaria, which is spread by the bites of infected mosquitos. This disease, which was known as ague, affected parts of Europe until the 19th century.

---

2. How are Third World diseases often spread?

---

3. Give some examples of diseases which kill many children in the Third World but not in developed countries. What causes the difference?

---

4. To what extent are health and illness a matter of choice?

Chapter 22 Medicine and choice in the modern world

Medicine is closely linked to religion, morals, social change and politics. We have already seen how links of this sort can have an effect on medical progress. Sometimes progress is hindered or stopped; at other times it is helped and encouraged.

Frequently, people disagree about changes in medicine: some say a certain change is good; others say it is wicked and evil. In the last hundred years, doctors and medical scientists have found new methods of *contraception* (birth control). To some extent, they have done this because of social and political pressures, such as women's desire for greater control of their lives and their bodies. However, people have argued fiercely about the new methods – and also about the whole idea of birth control. Similarly, new means of *abortion* have led to fierce discussion about the rights and wrongs of destroying a *foetus* (an unborn child). Some people say that abortion is really a form of murder. Others say this about *euthanasia* (mercy killing).

Taking part in a demonstration about abortion. Which side are these men and women on?

Accepting death

There are cases where doctors knowingly hasten a patient's death without really practising euthanasia. They may do this when they give powerful pain-killing drugs to those who are dying. It is known that such drugs can shorten life. However, since the doctor's main (or official) purpose is to combat pain no one suggests that he or she is doing wrong.

In other cases, a person may be unconscious and without any hope of recovery. Is there any point in keeping that person alive for years with drugs and machines? Often, with the family's agreement, treatment is stopped, and this allows natural death to occur. As with abortion and euthanasia, a choice is made between life and death, and this raises all sorts of difficult questions. Once again, the questions have more to do with religion than medicine. If people believe that death leads to some sort of after-life they may be ready to die or allow a loved-one to die. If not, they may hang on to life, hoping for a cure to conditions that cannot be cured at the moment.

A few people have themselves or their relatives frozen and stored when they die. They hope that advances in medical skill will permit them to be revived and cured at a later date. Such hopes could affect the future progress of medical science, especially if wealthy people leave money to pay for research.

1. Discuss some of the ways in which religion and the Church have influenced medicine. Have the effects been mainly good or mainly bad?

Problems of cost

Some new forms of treatment are very expensive, and doctors are sometimes forced to let certain patients die while others with the same disease are treated and cured. Would this problem be solved if nations spent more money on health? Should they begin by providing water and very cheap medicines for those in the poorest parts of the world?

Organ transplants

Organ transplants are one of the new and very expensive forms of treatment. Most organs come from people who have recently died in accidents. Doctors need fresh organs for transplanting and some people think they may accidentally take an organ from someone who is not quite dead. Deciding exactly when death occurs is one of the most difficult problems in medicine.

Transplants can raise moral problems too. According to a writer called Rattray Taylor, a person might one day introduce someone with the following words:

> 'I want you to meet my uncle and niece. They were in a car smash but fortunately the surgeon was able to get one complete body out of the damaged bits . . . '

Religious and moral objections mean that few law codes permit euthanasia. This is an example of how religion and morals affect what doctors are able to do. (Their own religious or moral feelings will also be extremely important.) Restrictions on euthanasia may have a positive side. For example, they probably encourage progress in pain control and the care of the dying.

Media attention for a heart transplant patient.

Where should we stop?

How far should doctors go in helping childless couples to have a baby? An egg is sometimes removed from a woman, fertilised and then replaced. Some people think that this can lead to doctors interfering with nature too much. They fear that doctors may one day decide which sort of person ought to be born. Would it be right to experiment with human *embryos* (fertilised eggs)? And can it be right to use helpless people or animals for experiments or as sources of serum? As you know, the use of animals up to the present has helped in developing vaccines and other forms of medicine. These days, many people oppose the scientific use of animals, especially when they suffer pain. Others say that animals must be used in testing new medicines and weapons. Would you object if soap or shampoo was tested in animals' eyes to find out whether it hurt? Would you object if bullets were shot at animals as a way of learning more about wounds? Would you refuse a dose of animal serum if it could save your life or the life of a friend?

Aids

A fatal disease called **aids** is spreading throughout the world. It is caused by a virus, and some people think it was made in an unwise experiment and then released by accident. Others think that the virus may have come from space. According to a newspaper,

> 'Aids has swept into our lives with a speed that has confounded science, shocked governments and frightened us all.'

Aids is passed on mainly by sexual intercourse. No cure has been found, but doctors are trying to stop **aids** from spreading. Some think compulsory screening is needed. Many infected people appear to be healthy, and doctors want to pick them out before they can pass the virus on. But is compulsory screening right? And would it be fair to restrict victims' lives in order to limit the spread of infection?

---

2. Look again at chapter 10. What similarities can you see between people's reaction to the Black Death and their reaction to aids? (This is something to think about and discuss. You may get ideas from reports in newspapers and on television.)

Glossary

abortion ending a pregnancy early, causing the developing child to die
acupuncture a form of treatment where the patient's flesh is pierced with needles
aesculapia temples where healings were carried out in ancient Greece
aids a fatal disease which began to spread in the 1970s. It is often passed on by sexual intercourse
alternative medicine unusual forms of medical treatment like acupuncture and homoepathy
anaesthetic a substance which makes a part of a patient's body numb, or which sends him/her to sleep so he cannot feel pain
anatomy what the body is like inside
antibiotics medicines which kill germs inside the body
antibodies cells in the blood which can kill a certain kind of germ
antiseptic a germ-killing substance
appendicitis infection of an organ called the appendix
artery a pipe which carries blood from the heart
arthritis a painful and crippling disease affecting the joints
bacteria germs
bile a substance which is made in the liver
Black Death the epidemic of plague which affected Europe in 1349
bleeding, blood-letting releasing some of a patient's blood in order to cure him/her
bowels the final part of a person's intestines
capillaries the narrowest blood-vessels, visible only with the aid of a microscope
cholera a disease causing diarrhoea and death
contraception birth control
cowpox a mild disease which milkmaids sometimes caught from cows
cupping a way of letting blood
diagnosis working out the meaning of symptoms to find what disease a patient is suffering from
dissection cutting up bodies (usually for the purpose of learning about anatomy)
embryo a fertilised egg in the early stage of development
epidemic an outbreak of disease affecting a very large number of people
epilepsy a disease of the brain which causes fits
euthanasia mercy-killing
faith-healing healing by means of faith (especially faith in God)
foetus an unborn child developing in its mother's womb
fracture a broken bone
gangrene decay affecting a wound or other part of the body
Hippocratic Oath the oath which doctors had to swear when they left the medical school at Cos
holistic medicine treatment and medical advice that are based on everything about the patient, such as his work, home-life, worries etc
homoeopathy treating symptoms with drugs that could cause the same symptoms if taken by someone in perfect health
humours blood, phlegm, yellow bile and black bile. The ancient Greeks thought health depended on having the right amounts in the body
hygiene health-care and cleanliness
infection disease caused by germs
infirmary a hospital; a small one attached to a monastery etc
kidney an organ which helps to purify blood. It produces urine
laxative a medicine or drug which relieves constipation
liver an organ which helps to purify blood
'magic bullet' a drug (especially an antibiotic) which does not have any side effects
malaria a disease which is spread by mosquito bites
malnutrition illness or weakness because of poor diet
mandrake a medicinal plant (now rarely used)
measles a disease which kills many children in poorer parts of the world
medicine the understanding and cure of diseases and injuries; a substance given to cure a patient or ease his symptoms
medicine man a witch doctor
microbes germs, bacteria
midwife someone who helps a woman to give birth
mummification an ancient way of preserving a body
nerve a special thread or cord in the body which carries messages
organ part of the body, such as the heart or the liver
paralysis inability to move due to illness or injury
parasite a creature (such as a flea) which feeds on the blood or flesh of a larger living animal
penicillin the most important antibiotic
phlegm mucus (a yellowy substance) coughed up from the lungs
physiology the way the various organs work
placebo a dummy pill which satisfies a patient that he or she is being treated
plague a serious disease often spread by fleas from rats
plasma the liquid which is left after blood has clotted
pleurisy inflammation of the outer lining of the lungs
prescription a recipe for making medicine; a doctor's note saying what sort of medicine a patient should have
preventive medicine ways of preventing illness from starting
pulse a patient's heart-beat (often felt at his wrist)
pus the yellow stuff from a boil or infected wound
quarantine a period during which someone is kept away from others to stop him or her spreading infectious diseases
rabies a fatal disease which humans catch from infected dogs
salvarsan a drug used in treating syphilis
screening checking people for illness before they show any symptoms
serum medicine made from the plasma of blood
shock symptoms (such as a weak, rapid heart-beat) caused by pain or serious accident
side effect the unwanted effect which a drug may have
smallpox a disease which is now extremely rare due to vaccination
splint a rod or narrow board which is used to keep a limb straight while a bone heals.
spontaneous generation the idea that living things can come into existence by themselves, rather than being born etc.
sterilization the killing of all germs (for example, on a surgeon's tools); treatment given to ensure that someone can never have children
sulphonamides a family of drugs
suppuration festering
surgery treatment involving cutting a patient's body
symptom one of the signs of an illness
syphilis a disease spread by sexual intercourse
Third World the poor, undeveloped parts of the world
transplant the 'planting' of a healthy organ in a patient's body
trepanning removing a piece of a person's skull as part of primitive medical treatment
urine the liquid made by the kidneys
vaccine weakened germs (or viruses) used to protect a patient from a certain disease
varicose vein a diseased vein which is swollen with blood
vein a pipe which carries blood towards the heart
virus disease-causing life-form even smaller than bacteria
witch docter someone who tries to cure illness by magic, especially in a primitive tribe
x-ray a sort of ray which doctors can use to photograph the inside of the body
zodiac chart an astrological chart showing dates when operations should *not* be attempted